ESTATE PLANNING FOR BEGINNERS

ESTATE PLANNING FOR BEGINNERS

A COMPREHENSIVE GUIDE TO ASSET PROTECTION, BENEFICIARY MANAGEMENT, AND SECURING YOUR LEGACY

FINANCIAL PLANNING ESSENTIALS
BOOK 2

CALVIN BOSWELL

Copyright © 2024 by Calvin Boswell

All rights reserved. No part of this book may be reproduced, stored in a retrieval system, or transmitted in any form or by any means, electronic, mechanical, photocopying, recording, or otherwise, without the prior written permission of the publisher, Book Bound Studios.

The information contained in this book is based on the author's personal experiences and research. While every effort has been made to ensure the accuracy of the information presented, the author and publisher cannot be held responsible for any errors or omissions.

This book is intended for general informational purposes only and is not a substitute for professional medical, legal, or financial advice. If you have specific questions about any medical, legal, or financial matters, you should consult with a qualified healthcare professional, attorney, or financial advisor.

Book Bound Studios is not affiliated with any product or vendor mentioned in this book. The views expressed in this book are those of the author and do not necessarily reflect the views of Book Bound Studios.

To all who stand at tomorrow's threshold, uncertain yet hopeful. This book is dedicated to you—the beginners, the planners, the dreamers. May you find within these pages the knowledge to secure your legacy, the courage to face the unknown, and the wisdom to cherish every moment. Let this guide be your beacon, illuminating the path to a future where your dreams and the well-being of your loved ones are safeguarded. Here's to building a lasting legacy, one thoughtful step at a time.

Planning is bringing the future into the present so that you can do something about it now.

— ALAN LAKEIN

CONTENTS

Introduction to Estate Planning   xiii

1. UNDERSTANDING YOUR ASSETS   1
   Identifying Your Assets   1
   Valuing Your Assets   3
   Types of Ownership   4
   Digital Assets   6
   Business Interests   8
   Chapter Summary   9

2. YOUR BENEFICIARIES   11
   Defining Your Beneficiaries   11
   Special Considerations for Minor Children   13
   When Beneficiaries Have Special Needs   14
   Managing Potential Conflicts Among Beneficiaries   15
   Charitable Bequests   17
   Chapter Summary   18

3. WILLS AND TRUSTS   21
   The Role of a Will in Estate Planning   21
   Types of Trusts   23
   Choosing Between a Will and a Trust   25
   The Process of Creating a Will   27
   How Trusts Can Manage and Protect Assets   28
   Chapter Summary   30

4. TAXES AND ESTATE PLANNING   33
   Understanding Estate Taxes   33
   Gift Taxes and How They Affect Estate Planning   35
   Strategies to Minimize Taxes   36
   State Estate and Inheritance Taxes   38
   The Role of Life Insurance in Estate Taxes   40
   Chapter Summary   41

5. HEALTHCARE DECISIONS AND ADVANCE
   DIRECTIVES 43
   Healthcare Power of Attorney 43
   Living Wills and Medical Directives 45
   Do Not Resuscitate Orders (DNR) 46
   The Importance of Communicating Your Wishes 48
   HIPAA Authorizations 49
   Chapter Summary 51

6. PROTECTING YOUR ESTATE 53
   Asset Protection Strategies 53
   Insurance as a Protective Measure 55
   The Role of Liability Coverage 56
   Homestead Protections 58
   Protecting Assets from Creditors 59
   Chapter Summary 61

7. THE ROLE OF EXECUTORS AND TRUSTEES 63
   Duties of an Executor 63
   Selecting an Executor 65
   Duties of a Trustee 66
   Selecting a Trustee 68
   Managing Estate and Trust Administration 70
   Chapter Summary 71

8. PLANNING FOR INCAPACITY 73
   Financial Power of Attorney 73
   The Role of Conservatorships 75
   Managing Your Digital Legacy 76
   Chapter Summary 77

9. ESTATE PLANNING FOR BUSINESS OWNERS 79
   Assessing Your Business Assets 79
   Buy-Sell Agreements 81
   Succession Planning 83
   Insurance for Business Owners 84
   Transferring Ownership and Control 86
   Chapter Summary 88

10. KEEPING YOUR ESTATE PLAN CURRENT 89
   When to Review Your Estate Plan 89
   Life Events that Affect Your Estate Plan 91
   Updating Beneficiaries 92
   Revising Legal Documents 94
   The Impact of Law Changes on Your Estate Plan 96
   Chapter Summary 97

   The Legacy You Leave Behind 99

   Your Feedback Matters 107
   About the Author 109

INTRODUCTION TO ESTATE PLANNING

What is Estate Planning?

Estate planning might evoke images of grand mansions and vast fortunes, but it's not just for the wealthy. It's a process that allows anyone, regardless of their financial status, to set out instructions for managing and distributing their assets after they pass away. It also encompasses decisions about your healthcare and financial affairs should you become unable to make them yourself.

At its core, estate planning is about ensuring that your wishes are honored, your loved ones are provided for, and your legacy is preserved according to your design, not left to the state's default rules. It's a comprehensive approach that includes drafting legal documents like wills, trusts, powers of attorney, and healthcare directives. Each serves a specific purpose, from designating heirs and beneficiaries to appoint someone to decide on your behalf if you're incapacitated.

Estate planning is not a one-time event but an ongoing process. Your estate plan should evolve as life changes—marriages, divorces, births, deaths, and changes in the law. It's about maintaining control over your affairs, protecting your assets, and providing peace of mind for you and those you care about.

By creating a thoughtful estate plan, you can avoid leaving your heirs with the potential burden of probate, minimize taxes and legal fees, and prevent family disputes. It's a way to ensure that your story—your values, care for your family, and charitable inclinations—is told how you want it to be.

Essentially, estate planning is a deeply personal yet universally important process. It's about making clear and legally recognized decisions that reflect your wishes and protect your most cherished assets—your family and your legacy.

The Importance of Estate Planning

Having explored the basics of estate planning, it's crucial to understand why dedicating time and resources to this process is beneficial and essential. At its core, estate planning is about securing peace of mind for yourself and ensuring that your loved ones are provided for in your absence. It's a proactive approach to managing your assets and legacy, essential for several reasons.

Firstly, estate planning allows you to maintain control over your assets. Without a plan, state laws determine how your assets are distributed after passing. This may not align with your wishes or the needs of your beneficiaries. Creating an estate plan ensures that your assets go exactly where you want them to—to family, friends, or charitable organizations.

Secondly, estate planning can significantly reduce the stress and burden on your family during a difficult time. The loss of a loved one is an emotional ordeal, and the added pressure of sorting out financial and legal matters can be overwhelming. An estate plan provides clear instructions on handling your affairs, which can alleviate potential conflicts and confusion among your heirs.

Another important aspect of estate planning is the potential to minimize taxes and other expenses. With the right strategies in place, you can reduce the amount of your estate that goes to taxes, legal fees, and court costs, thereby maximizing the value of the inheritance you leave behind.

Furthermore, estate planning is not only about the distribution of assets; it also encompasses decisions about your care should you become incapacitated. Through powers of attorney and healthcare directives, you can appoint someone you trust to manage your finances and make medical decisions if you cannot.

Lastly, estate planning is an ongoing process. Life changes—such as marriage, divorce, the birth of children, and the acquisition of new assets—mean your estate plan should evolve to reflect your current circumstances and goals. Regularly reviewing and updating your plan ensures it remains effective and aligned with your intentions.

Essentially, estate planning is a fundamental step in managing your personal affairs. It's about taking charge of your future, protecting your assets, and caring for the people you love. With the right plan, you can leave a lasting, positive impact beyond your lifetime.

Common Misconceptions

As we delve into estate planning, clearing the fog of misconceptions surrounding this critical process is crucial. Many people approach estate planning with preconceived notions that may hinder their ability to plan effectively for the future. Let's dispel some of these myths to set a solid foundation for your understanding.

Firstly, there's a common belief that estate planning is only for the wealthy. This couldn't be further from the truth. Regardless of the size of your assets, estate planning is about ensuring that what you own is transferred according to your wishes and in the most efficient manner possible. It's about protecting your loved ones and ensuring that unnecessary taxes or legal fees do not erode the fruits of your labor.

Another widespread misconception is that estate planning solely distributes assets after death. A comprehensive estate plan also addresses your needs while you're alive. It includes directives for managing your finances and healthcare decisions if you need help to do so yourself. Often overlooked, this aspect of estate planning is as vital as planning for asset distribution.

Many beginners also mistakenly think that once an estate plan is created, it's set in stone. The truth is that estate planning is an ongoing process. Life changes—such as marriage, divorce, the birth of a child, or the acquisition of new assets—necessitate updates to your estate plan to reflect your current situation and wishes.

Lastly, there's the myth that estate planning is too complex and expensive for the average person. While it's true that estate planning can be complex, it doesn't have to be prohibitively expensive. With the proper guidance and a step-by-step approach, you can create an estate plan that fits your needs without breaking the bank.

Understanding these misconceptions is the first step in recognizing the true nature and scope of estate planning. It's a process that is as personal as it is critical and accessible to everyone. With these myths out of the way, we can focus on the actual goals of estate planning, which will help you secure your legacy and provide for your loved ones in the best way possible.

Goals of Estate Planning

Having dispelled some common misconceptions about estate planning, we must focus on the core objectives that make this process so critical for individuals and families. At its essence, estate planning is a proactive approach to organizing your personal and financial affairs. The goals of estate planning are both varied and personal, but they typically include the following key objectives:

- **Distribution of Assets:** One of the primary goals of estate planning is to ensure that your assets are distributed according to your wishes after you pass away. Without a plan, state laws will determine how your assets are divided, which might not align with your preferences. A well-crafted estate plan allows you to designate beneficiaries for your assets, which can include family members, friends, or charitable organizations.
- **Protection of Loved Ones:** Estate planning is about assets and ensuring your loved ones are provided for and protected. This can mean setting up trusts for minor children or dependents with special needs, choosing guardians, or ensuring that a surviving spouse is financially secure.
- **Minimizing Taxes and Expenses:** A thoughtful estate plan can help minimize taxes, court costs, and legal fees. Utilizing various estate planning tools, such as trusts, you can reduce the estate tax burden on your heirs and preserve more of your estate for their benefit.
- **Avoiding Probate:** Probate is the legal process through which a deceased person's estate is properly distributed to heirs and designated beneficiaries, and any debt owed to creditors is paid off. It can be time-consuming and expensive. Many people aim to avoid probate through their estate planning efforts to expedite the distribution of their assets and reduce costs.
- **Planning for Incapacity:** Estate planning also addresses the possibility of your becoming incapacitated before death. Through powers of attorney and living wills, you can appoint someone to manage your financial affairs, make healthcare decisions, and communicate your wishes regarding life-sustaining treatment if you cannot do so yourself.

- **Charitable Intentions:** If you have philanthropic goals, estate planning can help you establish a legacy of giving. You can set up charitable trusts or make specific bequests in your will to support the causes and organizations that are important to you.
- **Business Succession:** For business owners, estate planning is crucial for the continuation or orderly succession of the business. It involves planning for the transition of ownership and management to ensure the business continues to operate smoothly without you.
- **Peace of Mind:** Finally, one of the most significant goals of estate planning is to provide peace of mind for you and your loved ones. Knowing that you have a plan articulating your wishes can alleviate stress and potential conflicts among those you leave behind.

As we move forward, we will delve into the estate planning process, providing a roadmap for creating a comprehensive plan that aligns with these goals. The process involves several steps, from taking inventory of your assets to executing the necessary legal documents, and each step is designed to help you achieve a secure and intentional plan for your legacy.

Overview of the Estate Planning Process

Having established the fundamental goals of estate planning in the previous section, it's time to delve into the estate planning process. This journey is not just about drafting documents; it's about creating a roadmap for the future that reflects your wishes and provides for your loved ones. The process can be intricate, but it becomes manageable and less daunting with a step-by-step approach.

Firstly, let's begin with taking stock of your assets. This includes everything you own—real estate, bank accounts, investments, retirement funds, insurance policies, and personal property. Having a clear picture of what you have is essential because this will form the basis of your estate plan.

Next, consider your beneficiaries. These are the people or entities you want to inherit your assets. You are deciding who gets what, which is a personal decision that should be made carefully. It's also essential to consider alternate beneficiaries if your primary choices cannot be inherited.

Once you've identified your assets and beneficiaries, it's time to think about how you want to distribute your assets. This involves making decisions about who gets what and when. For example, you might want some beneficiaries to receive their inheritance outright. In contrast, others might receive theirs through a trust that provides for more controlled distribution.

Another critical component is selecting fiduciaries—individuals you trust to fulfill your wishes. This includes an executor of your will, a trustee if you establish a trust, and agents for financial and healthcare powers of attorney. These roles are pivotal, as these people will be responsible for managing your estate and making decisions on your behalf if you cannot do so.

With these decisions in mind, it's time to create the legal documents to ensure your wishes are honored. The most common documents in an estate plan include a will, a durable power of attorney for finances, a healthcare power of attorney, and often a trust. Each serves a unique purpose and works together to form a comprehensive estate plan.

After drafting these documents, reviewing them regularly and updating them as your life circumstances change is crucial. Marriage, divorce, the birth of children or grandchildren, and significant changes in financial status are all events that should trigger a review of your estate plan.

Lastly, it's essential to communicate your plans to your loved ones. While it might be a difficult conversation, it's essential to ensure that your wishes are understood and that your family knows where to find your important documents when the time comes.

Remember, estate planning is not a one-time event but an ongoing process. As your life evolves, so too should your estate plan. By taking these steps, you can create a plan that provides peace of mind for you and security for your beneficiaries.

Chapter Summary

- Estate planning is for everyone, not just the wealthy, and involves managing assets and healthcare decisions.
- It includes creating wills, trusts, powers of attorney, and healthcare directives, and it should be updated with life changes.
- Estate planning ensures assets are distributed as desired, reduces family stress, minimizes taxes, and plans for incapacity.
- Common misconceptions include that it's only for the rich, it's only about death, it's set in stone, and it's too complex or expensive.
- Goals include asset distribution, protecting loved ones, minimizing taxes, avoiding probate, planning for incapacity, charitable giving, business succession, and peace of mind.
- The process involves inventorying assets, choosing beneficiaries, deciding asset distribution, selecting fiduciaries, and creating legal documents.
- Regular updates to the estate plan are necessary due to life changes, and communication with loved ones is crucial.
- Estate planning is an ongoing process that evolves with life's changes, providing security and peace of mind.

1

UNDERSTANDING YOUR ASSETS

Identifying Your Assets

Embarking on the estate planning journey can often feel like you're trying to navigate a maze without a map. But fear not! The first step to finding your path is identifying what you're bringing along for the journey—your assets. In this section, we'll explore the various types of assets you may have and how to compile a comprehensive list that will serve as the cornerstone of your estate plan.

Think of your assets as the building blocks of your financial life. They are the tangible and intangible items you own that have value. You'll want to create a clear and detailed inventory to get started. This list should be thorough, as it will be crucial for the next steps in your estate planning process.

Begin with the most apparent items: your real estate. This includes your home, vacation properties, rental properties, or land you own. Next, consider your personal property, including vehicles, jewelry, art, collectibles, and furniture. You can touch and feel these items, and they often carry both sentimental and monetary value.

Moving on to financial assets, this category includes the contents of your bank accounts—checking, savings, and certificates of deposit. It also covers investments like stocks, bonds, mutual funds, and retirement accounts such as IRAs and 401(k)s. Don't overlook life insurance policies and annuities, which can be significant financial resources for your beneficiaries.

Business owners will need to include their business interests. Whether you own a small family business or a share of a larger enterprise, these interests are a vital part of your asset portfolio.

Lastly, consider any intellectual property you own, such as patents, copyrights, or trademarks. These can be valuable assets, especially if they generate ongoing royalties or have the potential for future monetization.

As you compile this list, remember to include digital assets as well. In our increasingly online world, these can range from social media accounts to cryptocurrency holdings and even domain names you own.

Once you have a comprehensive list, you'll have a clearer picture of what you own—a crucial step before you can effectively plan for how these assets will be managed during your life and distributed after your passing. With this inventory in hand, you'll be ready to move on to the next phase: valuing your assets, which is essential for understanding the potential tax implications and making informed decisions about your estate.

Valuing Your Assets

Now that you've identified your assets, the next crucial phase in estate planning is understanding their value. Valuing your assets is not just about knowing their current market price; it's about recognizing the economic worth they hold for you and your beneficiaries. This valuation will serve as a cornerstone for various decisions in your estate planning journey, including tax planning, distribution of assets, and ensuring your loved ones are taken care of according to your wishes.

To begin with, let's consider liquid assets. These are the assets that can be easily converted into cash. Examples include savings accounts, stocks, bonds, and mutual funds. The value of these assets is generally straightforward to determine. You can look at your latest account statements or check the current market prices for stocks and bonds. Keeping these valuations current is essential, as they can fluctuate with market conditions.

Next, we have real estate, which includes your home, any rental properties, or land you own. Valuing real estate can be more complex due to location, condition, market trends, and property improvements. Consider consulting with a professional appraiser or looking at recent sales of comparable properties in your area for an accurate assessment.

Personal property, such as vehicles, jewelry, art, and collectibles, must also be valued. Resources like Kelley Blue Book can reasonably estimate everyday items like cars. However, for items like art or antiques, you might need a professional appraisal to understand their market value, especially if they are rare or have historical significance.

Business interests present another layer of complexity. Determining its value can be intricate if you own a business or a share of one. It may involve analyzing the company's financial statements, considering its earning potential, and obtaining a professional business valuation.

Retirement accounts, including IRAs and 401(k)s, are valued based on the current statements provided by the financial institutions managing these accounts. Remember that these types of accounts may have tax implications that affect their value to your beneficiaries.

Lastly, life insurance policies are unique assets. Their value to your estate is not the cash surrender value but the death benefit your beneficiaries will receive. This amount should be considered in the overall valuation of your assets, as it can significantly impact your estate's liquidity upon your passing.

In valuing your assets, it's also essential to consider any debts or liabilities against them, as these will affect the net value of your estate. Mortgages, loans, and credit card debts must be subtracted from the asset values to get a clear picture of your net worth.

Remember, valuing your assets is not a one-time task. It's a dynamic process that should be revisited regularly or when significant life events occur. Keeping your asset valuations current will ensure that your estate plan remains relevant and practical, reflecting your actual financial situation at any given time.

By understanding the value of your assets, you are better equipped to make informed decisions about how to structure your estate plan. This clarity will help you in the following steps, where you'll consider the implications of different types of ownership and how they can affect the transfer of your assets.

Types of Ownership

In estate planning, understanding the types of ownership tied to your assets is as crucial as knowing their value. Ownership dictates who can use, manage, and ultimately inherit these assets, so it's essential to grasp the different forms of ownership and how they may affect your estate plan.

To start, let's talk about sole ownership. This is the simplest form: if you own an asset in your name alone, you have complete control over it. This includes the right to sell, gift, or bequeath the asset as you see fit. Common examples of sole ownership include personal items, a car, or a bank account that doesn't have a designated beneficiary or co-owner.

Next, joint ownership involves sharing control of an asset with one or more individuals. The most common type of joint ownership is joint tenancy with right of survivorship. If one owner passes away, their asset share automatically passes to the surviving owner(s), bypassing the probate process. This is often used for real estate, bank accounts, and other significant assets.

Another form of joint ownership is tenancy in common, where each owner has a distinct, divisible interest in the asset. Unlike joint tenancy, there's no right of survivorship; when one owner dies, their share becomes part of their estate and is distributed according to their will or state law if there's no will.

For married couples, some states recognize tenancy by the entirety, which is similar to joint tenancy but adds a layer of protection against creditors and allows ownership to transfer seamlessly to the surviving spouse.

Then there's community property, a concept that applies in some states, primarily in the western United States. In these jurisdictions, assets acquired during a marriage are considered jointly owned by both spouses, regardless of whose name is on the title. This can significantly affect estate planning, as each spouse claims half of the community property.

Understanding the nuances of these ownership types is more than just academic; it directly impacts how you plan for the future of your assets. For instance, assets owned jointly with the right of survivorship will not be part of your probate estate so that they won't be distributed according to your will. This can be a blessing and a potential source of conflict if it's different from what you intended.

Considering these ownership types, it's also important to recognize that designations like beneficiaries on life insurance policies and retirement accounts can override what's written in your will. These designations are a form of "payable on death" ownership, where the asset passes directly to the named beneficiary.

In the digital age, it's also vital to consider the ownership of digital assets, which can include everything from social media accounts to digital currencies. But we'll delve deeper into that topic in the next section.

For now, take stock of your assets and consider their value and how they're owned. This will guide how you structure your estate plan to ensure that your assets are distributed according to your wishes and that the process is as smooth and conflict-free as possible for your heirs.

Digital Assets

In the digital age, your estate is no longer limited to tangible assets like real estate, vehicles, or family heirlooms. A significant and often overlooked component of modern estate planning is the management of digital assets. These are the electronic records and files you own or control, and they can range from the sentimental to the financially significant.

To begin with, consider your digital assets. These may include digital photographs, videos, social media accounts, and personal emails. While they might not hold monetary value, they are often rich in sentimental value and an integral part of your digital legacy. Deciding what should happen to these personal digital assets after you pass away is an essential step in estate planning. You should designate a digital executor, someone you trust to handle your digital presence according to your wishes.

Next, there are digital assets with clear financial value. These could be your online banking accounts, investment portfolios, and cryptocurrency holdings. As you would with traditional financial assets, ensuring that your beneficiaries have the necessary information to access these digital funds is crucial. However, unlike traditional assets, digital ones may require specific usernames, passwords, and even two-factor authentication methods to access.

Moreover, you may own digital business assets if you're an entrepreneur or involved in online business activities. These include domain names, online stores, blogs, and associated revenue streams. These assets can be significant and may require special consideration to transfer ownership or control as part of your estate.

Intellectual property in digital form, such as ebooks, digital music, and software you've created, also falls under this category. These assets can continue to generate income beyond your lifetime, so it's essential to establish who will control and benefit from them.

When planning for your digital assets, compiling a comprehensive inventory is essential. This list should include details such as the type of asset, where it's located, and how to access it. Remember, laws governing access to digital assets after someone's death are still evolving. Hence, it's wise to consult an estate planning attorney knowledgeable about the digital realm.

Lastly, be aware of the terms of service agreements for your online accounts. Some platforms have specific policies for handling accounts after a user's death, which can affect how you plan for these assets.

By managing your digital assets, you ensure that your online life is as organized and respected as your physical one, providing peace of mind for you and clarity for your loved ones.

Business Interests

In the realm of estate planning, understanding the full scope of your assets is crucial. Among these assets, business interests often stand out as valuable and complex. Suppose you're an entrepreneur or a stakeholder in a business. In that case, these interests can form a significant part of your estate and require careful consideration to ensure they are managed according to your wishes after you pass away.

Business interests can range from sole proprietorships and partnerships to shares in a corporation or membership interests in a limited liability company (LLC). Each type of business interest has its own set of rules for succession and transferability, which company bylaws, shareholder agreements, and state laws can influence.

The business and the owner are legally considered one and the same for sole proprietorships. This means that the business does not continue to exist as a separate entity upon the owner's death. Instead, its assets and liabilities become part of the owner's estate. They are distributed according to their will or state intestacy laws if no will exists.

In the case of partnerships, the situation can be more complex. Unless a partnership agreement specifies what happens when a partner dies, the partnership may automatically dissolve. To prevent this, partners often have buy-sell agreements in place, which allow the surviving partners to purchase the deceased partner's interest, providing liquidity to the estate and continuity for the business.

For those with interests in corporations, mainly closely held corporations, the transfer of shares after death can be governed by shareholder agreements. These agreements often include provisions restricting the transfer of shares to maintain control within a particular group, such as family members or existing shareholders. They may also outline buy-sell provisions similar to those in partnerships.

Suppose you have an ownership stake in an LLC. In that case, the operating agreement is the crucial document that will dictate what happens to your membership interest upon your death. It's essential to review and understand the terms of the operating agreement, as they can vary widely from one LLC to another. Some may allow the interest to pass to heirs, while others may require that the interest be sold back to the LLC or the remaining members.

Regardless of your business interest, it's essential to have a clear succession plan in place. This plan should address who will take over the management of the business, how ownership interests will be transferred, and how the value of your business interests will be determined. It's also wise to consider the potential tax implications of transferring business interests, as they can be significant.

To ensure that your business interests are handled according to your wishes, it's advisable to work with an estate planning attorney who has experience with business succession planning. They can help you navigate the complexities of transferring business interests and integrate these plans into your overall estate strategy.

Remember, your business is a legacy that can provide for your family or chosen successors long after you're gone. With thoughtful planning, you can ensure that this legacy is preserved and that the transition of your business interests is as smooth and beneficial as possible for those you leave behind.

Chapter Summary

- Begin estate planning by identifying and listing all assets, including real estate, personal property, financial assets, business interests, and intellectual property.

- Include digital assets such as social media accounts and cryptocurrency in the inventory.
- Value assets by considering current market prices and professional appraisals and account for any debts against them.
- Regularly update asset valuations to reflect changes in market conditions or personal circumstances.
- Understand different types of asset ownership, such as sole ownership, joint tenancy, tenancy in common, and community property.
- Recognize that ownership types and beneficiary designations affect asset distribution after death.
- Manage digital assets by creating an inventory and providing access information while considering online platform policies.
- For business interests, understand succession and transfer rules, create a clear plan, and consult an estate planning attorney.

2

YOUR BENEFICIARIES

Defining Your Beneficiaries

Regarding estate planning, determining your beneficiaries is one of the most crucial steps. You designate these individuals or entities to receive your assets upon your passing. It's a decision that requires careful thought and clear articulation to ensure your wishes are fulfilled as intended.

Beneficiaries include family members, friends, charitable organizations, or pets. They can be primary beneficiaries, who are first in line to receive your assets, or contingent beneficiaries, who will receive your assets if the primary beneficiaries cannot do so.

To define your beneficiaries, you'll need to consider the nature of your relationships and the needs of each potential recipient. For example, you can provide for your spouse or domestic partner, children, siblings, or aging parents. It's also important to consider the financial implications for your beneficiaries, such as any potential tax burdens that your legacy might impose on them.

When selecting beneficiaries, be as specific as possible to avoid any ambiguity. Instead of simply stating "my children" as beneficiaries, list their full names and other identifying information to clarify your intentions. This specificity is crucial to prevent disputes among family members and ensure your assets are distributed according to your wishes.

It's also wise to review and update your beneficiary designations periodically, especially after significant life events such as marriage, divorce, the birth of a child, or the death of a loved one. Life changes can have significant implications for your estate plan, and keeping your beneficiary designations current will help to avoid unintended consequences.

Remember, your choices regarding your beneficiaries will have a lasting impact. Take the time to reflect on your relationships and the needs of those you care about. Consider speaking with an estate planning attorney who can provide guidance tailored to your unique circumstances and help you navigate the complexities of beneficiary designations. With careful planning and clear communication, you can create a legacy that reflects your values and intentions.

Special Considerations for Minor Children

As you embark on the estate planning journey, one of the most heartfelt considerations is the well-being of your minor children. It's natural to want to ensure they are cared for and financially secure in your absence. However, leaving assets directly to children under the legal age of majority—typically 18 or 21, depending on your state—can complicate matters. Let's navigate these waters together to ensure your intentions for your children's future are met with care and legal prudence.

Firstly, it's essential to understand that minors cannot legally own substantial property in their names. Suppose you pass away, leaving assets directly to a minor without any legal arrangements. In that case, the court will appoint a guardian to manage those assets until the child reaches adulthood. This process can be time-consuming and expensive and may result in something other than your chosen person.

To avoid these complications, consider establishing a trust for your minor children. A trust lets you set terms for how and when the assets will be distributed. You can appoint a trustee whom you trust to manage the assets according to your instructions. This could include stipulations for education expenses, health care, living costs, and even distributions at certain ages or milestones.

Another option is to use the Uniform Transfers to Minors Act (UTMA) or Uniform Gifts to Minors Act (UGMA) accounts. These accounts allow you to transfer assets to a custodian who will manage them for the benefit of the minor until they reach a certain age—often 18 or 21. While more straightforward than a trust, these accounts offer less control over how the funds are used once the child reaches the age of majority.

Life insurance policies also require special consideration. Suppose you name your minor children as beneficiaries. In that case, the proceeds may be subject to the same issues as other assets left directly to them. Instead, you can name a trust as the policy's beneficiary, ensuring the proceeds are managed according to your terms.

Lastly, it's crucial to select a guardian for your minor children in your will. If you're not there, this person will care for your children's daily needs. While this decision is deeply personal and challenging, it's one of the most significant acts of love. It cares you can provide for your children.

Remember, the goal of estate planning is not just to pass on what you own but to pass on your values and provide for your loved ones according to your wishes. By considering these special considerations for your minor children, you're creating a framework that supports their growth and well-being, even when you're not there to guide them.

When Beneficiaries Have Special Needs

When planning your estate, it's crucial to consider the unique needs of any beneficiaries with disabilities or special needs. This consideration is not just a matter of sensitivity; it's about ensuring that the support you provide through your estate doesn't inadvertently disqualify them from essential government benefits or services they may receive.

Firstly, understand that direct inheritance can sometimes do more harm than good. For instance, if a beneficiary with special needs receives Supplemental Security Income (SSI) or Medicaid, an inheritance could increase their assets to a level that exceeds eligibility thresholds. This could result in a loss of benefits that are critical to their well-being.

To navigate this, many turn to a tool known as a Special Needs Trust (SNT). This type of trust allows you to leave assets for the benefit of a person with special needs without those assets being counted against them for eligibility purposes. The trust is managed by a trustee who disburses funds to cover costs that government benefits do not, such as personal care attendants, out-of-pocket medical expenses, or education services.

When setting up an SNT, it's essential to choose a trustworthy and knowledgeable trustee who is aware of the beneficiary's needs and government benefits rules. This person will have significant discretion over the trust's assets and must be able to manage them in a way that continues to protect the beneficiary's eligibility for aid.

Another consideration is the use of a letter of intent. While not legally binding, this document provides a detailed overview of the beneficiary's preferences, routines, medical needs, and other important information. It guides trustees and future caregivers to ensure the beneficiary's quality of life is maintained according to your wishes.

Lastly, updating your estate plan is essential as laws and circumstances change. Regular reviews with an attorney specializing in special needs planning can help ensure that your estate plan continues to serve the best interests of your beneficiaries with special needs.

Remember, thoughtful planning is the cornerstone of providing for a special-needs beneficiary. It's not just about the assets you leave behind but also about the structures and guidance you put in place to ensure those assets improve the quality of life for your loved ones without unintended consequences.

Managing Potential Conflicts Among Beneficiaries

Estate planning is not just about ensuring your assets are distributed according to your wishes; it's also about maintaining harmony among those you leave behind. As we delve into managing potential conflicts among beneficiaries, we must remember that emotions can run high regarding inheritance matters. Taking proactive steps can minimize disputes and ensure your legacy is peaceful rather than discord.

Firstly, clear communication is critical. It's advisable to discuss your estate plan with your beneficiaries while you can. This doesn't mean you need to divulge every detail, but explaining the reasoning behind your decisions can help prevent misunderstandings later on. If you've made unequal distributions, for instance, explaining that you've done so because one child has a greater financial need or has already provided substantial support to another can help mitigate feelings of favoritism or neglect.

Secondly, consider using a no-contest clause in your will or trust. This clause states that if a beneficiary challenges the estate plan and loses, they will receive nothing. While this can be a powerful deterrent to legal battles, it could be more foolproof and sometimes fuel the fire if beneficiaries feel coerced. It's essential to weigh the pros and cons of such a clause and to consult with an estate planning attorney to determine its effectiveness and legality in your jurisdiction.

Another strategy is to appoint an impartial executor or trustee. This should be someone who is not a beneficiary and can manage your estate objectively. The role of the executor is to administer your estate according to your wishes, and having someone who does not have a personal stake in the outcome can reduce the potential for conflict.

Additionally, consider creating a personal property memorandum. This document outlines who should receive specific items of sentimental or monetary value. It can be updated easily without changing your will or trust, allowing you to adapt to changing circumstances or relationships. By being specific about who gets what, you can avoid disputes over personal belongings, often the source of significant conflict among heirs.

Lastly, setting up a trust can be wise for those with significant assets. Trusts can provide a structured way to distribute your assets over time, which can be particularly helpful if you're concerned about a beneficiary's spending habits or want to provide for them in a way that doesn't involve a lump sum. Trusts can also offer privacy and avoid the probate process, which can be lengthy and contentious.

In conclusion, while it's impossible to predict every outcome, taking these steps can go a long way in preventing conflicts among your beneficiaries. By being thoughtful and thorough in your estate planning, you can help ensure that your legacy is preserved and that your loved ones are provided for in a way that promotes harmony rather than discord. Remember, the ultimate goal is to provide for your beneficiaries in a manner that aligns with your values and wishes while also considering their individual needs and relationships with one another.

Charitable Bequests

After ensuring that your loved ones are cared for in estate planning, consider leaving a lasting legacy through charitable bequests. This is a way to support causes and organizations close to your heart, even after you're gone.

Charitable bequests are gifts made as part of your will or trust that designate a portion of your estate to a charity or nonprofit organization. These gifts can take various forms, such as a specific dollar amount, a percentage of your estate, or particular assets. They can also be contingent upon certain conditions being met, such as the survival of other beneficiaries.

One of the primary benefits of including charitable bequests in your estate plan is the potential for tax relief. Charitable gifts can reduce the value of your estate for estate tax purposes, which can be significant if your estate exceeds the federal estate tax exemption amount. Additionally, if you have a taxable estate, these endowments can reduce or even eliminate the estate tax liability.

When selecting a charity for a legacy, it's essential to do your due diligence. Ensure that the organization is a qualified 501(c)(3) charity, which means that the IRS has recognized it as a tax-exempt organization. This status is crucial for the tax benefits of your legacy to be realized. You can verify an organization's status through the IRS website or request a copy of their determination letter.

It's also wise to be specific in your will or trust about which charity you want to benefit and how you want the funds to be used. If you have a particular program or purpose, stipulate this in your estate documents. This can help prevent ambiguity and ensure your charitable goals are met.

Discuss your intentions with the charity beforehand if you consider a significant gift. Many organizations have planned giving departments that can work with you to ensure your bequest is used according to your wishes. They can also provide specific language to include in your will or trust to facilitate the gift.

Remember, charitable bequests are not just for the wealthy. Even modest gifts can substantially impact an organization and its work. Plus, giving charitably can set a powerful example for your heirs, inspiring them to continue a legacy of generosity.

In conclusion, charitable bequests are a meaningful way to extend your influence and values beyond your lifetime. By thoughtfully integrating these gifts into your estate plan, you can support the causes you care about while reaping potential tax benefits and shaping how you are remembered. As with all aspects of estate planning, consulting with an estate planning attorney is advisable to ensure that your charitable intentions are clearly articulated and legally sound.

Chapter Summary

- Estate planning involves carefully choosing beneficiaries, such as family, friends, charities, or pets, to receive assets after one's passing.

- Beneficiaries can be primary or contingent; specificity in naming them helps avoid disputes and ensures wishes are followed.
- Regularly updating beneficiary designations, especially after significant life events, is essential to prevent unintended consequences.
- For minor children, consider trusts or custodial accounts to manage assets until adulthood and select a guardian for their care.
- When beneficiaries have special needs, use a Special Needs Trust (SNT) to provide for them without jeopardizing government benefits.
- To prevent beneficiary conflicts, communicate estate plans clearly, use no-contest clauses judiciously, and appoint an impartial executor.
- Charitable bequests can reduce estate taxes and support causes important to the benefactor, ensuring the charity is a qualified 501(c)(3) organization.
- Estate planning should reflect one's values and intentions, and consulting with an estate planning attorney can help navigate the complexities involved.

3

WILLS AND TRUSTS

The Role of a Will in Estate Planning

Regarding estate planning, one of the most fundamental tools at your disposal is a will. In its simplest form, a will is a legal document that outlines your wishes regarding the distribution of your assets and the care of any minor children upon your death. It is the cornerstone of a primary estate plan and serves as your voice to express your intentions when you are no longer here.

The role of a will in estate planning cannot be overstated. It provides instructions for managing and distributing your estate, including everything you own—your home, car, bank accounts, personal possessions, and more. Without a will, these decisions fall to state laws, which may not align with your wishes or the needs of your beneficiaries.

One of the primary benefits of having a will is the ability to choose an executor. You designate This person to carry out the instructions in your will, manage your estate, settle debts, and distribute your assets as directed. Choosing a trusted individual as your executor ensures your estate is handled according to your preferences.

Additionally, for those with minor children, a will is the vehicle through which you can appoint a guardian. This is one of the most critical decisions you can make, as it determines who will be responsible for raising your children if you cannot do so. Without a will, the court will decide who will take on this role, which may not coincide with your wishes.

It's also important to understand that a will does not cover certain assets. These include life insurance policies, retirement accounts, and assets held in joint tenancy or with designated beneficiaries. These pass outside the will directly to the named beneficiaries and are essential to your overall estate plan.

While a will is a powerful tool, it does have limitations. For instance, it does not provide any tax advantages. It cannot help your estate avoid probate—the legal process through which a will is validated, and your estate is settled. Probate can be time-consuming and costly, making your estate matter a public record matter.

For those seeking to manage their estate more privately or who wish to provide for their beneficiaries in a specific way, such as setting up conditional distributions or protecting assets from creditors, trusts can be an invaluable addition to a will. Trusts come in various forms and serve different purposes, which we will explore in detail in the following section. They can offer more control over your assets, potential tax benefits, and the ability to bypass the probate process, among other advantages.

In conclusion, a will is a critical element of any estate plan. It ensures that your wishes regarding the distribution of your assets and the care of your children are known and respected. However, it is just one part of a comprehensive estate plan, which may include tools like trusts to thoroughly address your needs and goals. Understanding a will's strengths and limitations helps you make informed decisions about protecting your legacy and providing for your loved ones.

Types of Trusts

As we delve into estate planning, we've already explored the significance of wills in ensuring your wishes are honored after you pass away. Now, let's shift our focus to trusts, another essential tool that can offer additional flexibility and control over managing and distributing your assets.

A trust is a fiduciary arrangement allowing a third party, or trustee, to hold assets on behalf of a beneficiary or beneficiary. Trusts can be arranged in many ways and specify how and when the assets pass to the beneficiaries. They come in various types, each with its own rules and purposes, and choosing the right one depends on your circumstances and goals.

- **Revocable Trusts**, also known as living trusts, are created during your lifetime and can be altered or revoked before death. They help avoid probate, the legal process of distributing your estate, which can be costly and time-consuming. With a revocable trust, you maintain control over the trust assets. You can act as the trustee, managing the property and assets held in the trust.

- **Irrevocable Trusts**, in contrast, cannot be modified or terminated without the beneficiary's permission after they are created. This type of trust can benefit estate tax considerations, as the assets placed into the trust are no longer considered part of your estate for tax purposes. It's a way to reduce your taxable estate, potentially shielding your beneficiaries from high taxes and providing asset protection from creditors.
- **Testamentary Trusts** are created as part of a will and only come into effect after your death. This type of trust allows you to set conditions for your assets' distribution. For example, you might stipulate that the assets should only be distributed once the beneficiary reaches a certain age or meets specific milestones, like college graduation.
- **Charitable Trusts** are set up to benefit a particular charity or the public. A charitable remainder trust, for instance, can provide an income stream to you or another beneficiary, with the remainder of the trust going to charity. Conversely, a charitable lead trust allows you to give a fixed amount to charity for several years, eventually passing the remaining assets to your beneficiaries.
- **Special Needs Trusts** are designed to benefit individuals with disabilities without disqualifying them from government assistance programs like Medicaid or Supplemental Security Income (SSI). These trusts can pay for expenses that enhance the beneficiary's quality of life while preserving their eligibility for public benefits.

- **Spendthrift Trusts** protect a beneficiary's inheritance from their potential creditors by prohibiting the beneficiary from selling or giving away their interest in the trust. It can also protect the assets from beneficiaries who might need to be financially savvy or prone to overspending.
- **Life Insurance Trusts** are irrevocable trusts that own a life insurance policy on your life. The death benefit from the policy can provide liquidity to your estate, pay estate taxes, or provide for your beneficiaries without the proceeds being subject to estate tax.

Understanding the nuances of each type of trust can be complex, but the effort is worthwhile. Trusts can offer a range of benefits, including tax advantages, asset protection, and ensuring that your wishes are carried out with precision. As you consider your estate planning options, consider your specific needs, the needs of your beneficiaries, and how different trusts might serve those needs. Remember, the right trust can be a powerful component of a comprehensive estate plan, working in concert with your will to achieve your ultimate goals.

Choosing Between a Will and a Trust

Regarding estate planning, one of the most critical decisions you'll make is whether to establish a will, a trust, or both. Understanding the differences between these two legal instruments and the unique benefits each offers is essential to making an informed choice that aligns with your circumstances and goals.

A will, also known as a testament, is a legal document articulating your wishes regarding the distribution of your assets and the care of any minor children upon your death. It is relatively straightforward to create and can effectively ensure that your estate is handled according to your preferences. One of the primary advantages of a will is its simplicity; it allows you to state clearly who gets what, and it can be updated as your situation changes. However, a will goes through probate, a public and often lengthy legal process where a court oversees the distribution of your estate. This can sometimes be costly and time-consuming for your heirs.

On the other hand, a trust is a more complex legal entity that can provide greater control over how your assets are managed and distributed, both during your lifetime and after your death. Trusts come in various types, as discussed in the previous section, and they can offer several advantages over wills. For instance, a trust can help your estate avoid probate, potentially saving time and maintaining privacy. Trusts can also provide tax benefits and protect your assets from creditors and legal judgments. Moreover, they can be structured to support beneficiaries over time, such as children or relatives with special needs, rather than providing a single lump-sum inheritance.

Choosing between a will and a trust—or deciding to use both—depends on multiple factors, including the size and complexity of your estate, your privacy concerns, your financial goals, and the needs of your potential heirs. A will might suffice if you have a smaller estate and straightforward wishes. A trust could be more appropriate for larger estates or more complex situations, such as owning property in multiple states or wanting to provide for a beneficiary with special needs.

It's also worth noting that the two are not mutually exclusive. Many people opt for a 'pour-over' will in conjunction with a trust. This will simply state that assets not already included in the trust should be transferred upon your death.

Ultimately, the choice between a will and a trust is personal and should be made carefully considering your unique situation. It's highly recommended to consult with an estate planning attorney who can guide you through the nuances of each option and help you craft a plan that best meets your needs and ensures your legacy is preserved as you intend.

As you move forward in your estate planning journey, the next step after deciding between a will and a trust is to understand the process of creating a will, which we will explore in the following section. This will give you a solid foundation to begin drafting this crucial document, should you choose it as part of your estate plan.

The Process of Creating a Will

Having decided that a will is the appropriate tool for your estate planning needs, the next step is understanding the process of creating a will. This document, often considered the cornerstone of an estate plan, outlines your wishes regarding the distribution of your assets and the care of any minor children after your passing. Let's walk through the steps to create a will, ensuring that your final wishes are honored and your loved ones are provided for according to your desires.

Step 1: Inventory Your Assets. Begin by making a comprehensive list of your assets. This includes your real estate properties, bank accounts, investment accounts, retirement funds, insurance policies, and personal property of value, such as jewelry, art, and vehicles. Also, consider digital assets such as online accounts or digital currencies. Knowing what you own is critical to effectively distributing your estate.

Step 2: Decide on Beneficiaries. After you've listed your assets, decide who will inherit them. Beneficiaries can include family members, friends, charitable organizations, or institutions. Be clear about who gets what, as ambiguity can lead to disputes among your heirs. If you have minor children, consider appointing a guardian to care for them.

Step 3: Choose an Executor. An executor is the person who will carry out the instructions of your will. Choose someone responsible and trustworthy, as this person will manage your estate's affairs, from paying off debts to distributing assets to your beneficiaries. It's also wise to name an alternate executor in case your first choice is unable or unwilling to serve.

Step 4: Draft Your Will. While it's possible to draft a will on your own, especially with online templates, working with an attorney is often advisable. A legal professional can ensure that your will complies with state laws and that your wishes are articulated. They can also help you navigate complex situations, such as providing for a special needs family member or structuring inheritances to minimize taxes.

Step 5: Sign Your Will in the Presence of Witnesses. For a will to be legally valid, it must be signed by at least two witnesses. These witnesses must be adults who are not beneficiaries of the will and can attest to your mental capacity when signing. Some states may also require the will to be notarized.

Step 6: Store Your Will Safely. Once signed, your will should be stored in a safe location, such as a fireproof safe or a safety deposit box. Ensure that your executor knows where to find your will and how to access it when the time comes. It's also a good idea to keep a list of your assets and their locations with the will for easier estate management.

Step 7: Review and Update as Necessary. Life changes such as marriage, divorce, the birth of children, or the acquisition of significant assets necessitate an update to your will. Review your will periodically and after major life events to reflect your wishes. Any changes should be made with the same formalities as the original will, including the signing and witnessing process.

Creating a will is a proactive step in managing your estate and can bring peace of mind to you and your loved ones. It's fundamental to ensuring that your legacy is passed on as you envision it. With your will in place, you can consider how trusts further enhance your estate planning strategy, offering additional layers of management and protection for your assets.

How Trusts Can Manage and Protect Assets

In estate planning, trusts emerge as a versatile tool, offering many benefits beyond the primary distribution of assets after one's passing. Trusts can be particularly effective for managing and protecting assets, both during one's lifetime and after. Understanding how trusts function and the advantages they provide is crucial for anyone looking to establish a comprehensive estate plan.

One of the primary ways trusts can manage assets is through their ability to set terms for how and when assets are distributed. This level of control is particularly beneficial for those who wish to provide for their beneficiaries over time rather than in a single lump sum. For instance, a trust can be set up to disburse funds when a beneficiary reaches certain milestones, such as college graduation or age.

Trusts also offer a degree of asset protection. By placing assets within a trust, they are generally shielded from creditors and legal judgments against the beneficiaries. This is because the assets are no longer considered the beneficiaries' personal property but rather the trust's property. This protection can be invaluable for beneficiaries at higher risk of legal action, such as professionals in litigious fields or individuals with significant debt.

Another protective feature of trusts is their ability to preserve privacy. Unlike wills, which become public documents once they go through probate, trusts typically do not. This means the details of your assets and whom you have chosen to benefit from them can remain private, away from the prying eyes of those outside the intended circle of trust beneficiaries and trustees.

For families with special needs individuals, trusts can be particularly beneficial. A special needs trust can be established to ensure that a beneficiary who receives government benefits will not be disqualified from such assistance due to an inheritance. The trust can provide supplemental resources without affecting the beneficiary's eligibility for public assistance programs.

Moreover, trusts can be used to manage and protect assets in the event of the trustor's incapacity. Through a living trust, you can appoint a trustee to manage your affairs without needing a court-appointed guardian or conservator should you become unable to manage your affairs. This can provide peace of mind, knowing that your assets are in trusted hands and that your wishes regarding their management will be respected.

In conclusion, trusts are a powerful component of estate planning that can offer significant advantages in managing and protecting assets. Whether your goal is to provide for your loved ones, protect your assets from creditors, or ensure privacy in the distribution of your estate, trusts can be tailored to meet those needs. As with any legal matter, it's wise to consult an estate planning attorney who can guide you through the intricacies of trust creation and help you determine the best type of trust for your circumstances.

Chapter Summary

- A will is a legal document that outlines asset distribution and care of minor children after death.
- State laws determine estate distribution without a will, which may not reflect personal wishes.
- Wills allow for the appointment of an executor and, for those with minor children, a guardian.
- A will does not cover certain assets like life insurance and retirement accounts.
- Wills do not offer tax benefits and do not avoid probate, which is public and can be costly.
- Trusts can be used alongside wills for more control, tax benefits, and bypass probate.

- Trusts come in various forms, such as revocable, irrevocable, testamentary, charitable, special needs, spendthrift, and life insurance trusts, each serving different purposes.
- Choosing between a will and a trust depends on individual circumstances, estate size, and complexity, with many opting for both to address different aspects of estate planning.

4

TAXES AND ESTATE PLANNING

Understanding Estate Taxes

When we talk about estate planning, one of the most critical aspects to understand is estate taxes. These are the taxes that your heirs may need to pay on the assets they inherit after you pass away. It's a common concern for many individuals who wish to leave as much as possible to their loved ones rather than to tax collectors.

Estate taxes, often called "death taxes," are levied by the federal government and, in some cases, state governments. The amount of tax due is calculated based on the estate's value at the time of the deceased's passing. It's important to note that not all estates are subject to estate taxes; there are exemption limits that change over time due to legislation and inflation adjustments.

As of the time of writing, the federal estate tax exemption is relatively high, meaning that only estates valued above a certain threshold are required to pay estate taxes. This exemption limit effectively removes the majority of estates from the federal estate tax's reach. However, the tax rate can be significant for those with assets exceeding this exemption amount, often rising to a substantial percentage of the estate's value.

It's also worth noting that some states have their own estate or inheritance taxes with different exemption levels and rates. Therefore, knowing the laws specific to your state is crucial when planning your estate.

One of the critical strategies in estate planning is to legally reduce the size of your taxable estate to minimize or avoid estate taxes. This can be done through various methods, such as making charitable donations, establishing trusts, or gifting assets during your lifetime. This leads us to gift taxes and their role in estate planning.

Gift taxes are closely related to estate taxes. They are a federal tax imposed on the transfer of property by gift during the giver's lifetime. The purpose of the gift tax is to prevent individuals from avoiding estate taxes by giving away their assets before they die. Just like estate taxes, there are annual and lifetime gift tax exemptions; understanding these can be a powerful tool in estate planning.

By making strategic gifts within these exemption limits, you can effectively transfer wealth to your beneficiaries. At the same time, you're still alive, reducing the value of your estate and potentially lowering the estate tax burden upon your death. However, it's essential to approach this carefully, as improper gifting can lead to unintended tax consequences.

In the next section, we'll delve deeper into how gift taxes work and how they can influence your estate planning strategy, ensuring you can make informed decisions that benefit you and your heirs.

Gift Taxes and How They Affect Estate Planning

As we delve into the intricacies of estate planning, it's crucial to understand not only the estate taxes discussed earlier but also the role of gift taxes and how they can influence your estate planning strategy. Gift taxes are a vital piece of the puzzle, and their implications can help you make more informed decisions about transferring wealth during your lifetime.

Gift taxes are federal taxes applied to transferring property or money to another person. At the same time, you are still alive without expecting to receive something of equal value in return. The key to gift taxes is a 'taxable gift.' Not all gifts are taxable, thanks to the annual gift tax exclusion. For instance, as of the time of writing, you can give up to $16,000 to any individual in a year without incurring a gift tax. If you're married, you and your spouse can each give $16,000, allowing for a combined gift of $32,000 to a single recipient without triggering the gift tax.

But what happens if you decide to be more generous and gift an amount that exceeds the annual exclusion? In that case, you'll need to file a gift tax return. However, filing a return doesn't necessarily mean you'll have to pay a tax. There's also a lifetime gift tax exemption that comes into play. This exemption is the total amount you can give away throughout your lifetime, above and beyond the annual exclusions, without paying gift taxes. The lifetime exemption amount is linked to the estate tax exemption, as they are part of the same tax system.

It's important to note that the gift and estate tax exemptions are unified. This means that the gifts you give during your lifetime that exceed the annual exclusion will reduce the amount you can leave tax-free at your death. For example, if you have a lifetime exemption of $11.7 million and make taxable gifts totaling $1 million during your lifetime, your remaining exemption that can be applied to your estate would be $10.7 million.

Understanding gift taxes is not just about knowing the numbers; it's about recognizing the opportunities and implications for your estate planning. For instance, making gifts within the annual exclusion limit can be a strategic way to reduce the size of your estate, potentially lowering estate taxes upon your death. Additionally, paying for someone's tuition or medical expenses directly to the institution can be exempt from gift taxes, which can be another effective way to pass on wealth without incurring taxes.

As you consider how to manage your estate, remember that the rules surrounding gift taxes can change due to legislation, so it's wise to stay informed or consult a professional. In the next part of our discussion, we'll explore various strategies that can help you minimize taxes and maximize the financial legacy you leave behind. By proactively managing gift taxes and understanding their relationship with estate taxes, you can craft a more effective and efficient estate plan that reflects your wishes and benefits your loved ones.

Strategies to Minimize Taxes

As we've seen, taxes can significantly impact your estate and the legacy you leave behind. Fortunately, there are several strategies you can employ to minimize the taxes levied on your estate. By understanding these tactics and incorporating them into your estate plan, you can ensure that more of your assets go to your loved ones rather than to tax collectors.

1. **Utilize the Annual Gift Tax Exclusion:** One of the simplest ways to reduce your estate tax liability is to give gifts during your lifetime. As per the current tax laws, you can give a certain amount

per year to as many individuals as you like without incurring gift tax. This reduces the size of your estate and allows you to see your beneficiaries enjoy their inheritance.

2. **Pay for Medical and Educational Expenses:** Besides the annual gift exclusion, payments made directly to a medical institution for someone's medical care or to an educational institution for tuition are exempt from gift tax. This can be a strategic way to support loved ones while decreasing your estate's value.

3. **Set Up Trusts:** Trusts can be a powerful tool in estate planning. Certain types of trusts, like irrevocable life insurance trusts, can remove the value of life insurance from your estate. Others, such as charitable remainder trusts, can provide income to beneficiaries before the remainder goes to a charity, which may also provide tax benefits.

4. **Take Advantage of the Marital Deduction:** If you are married, you can leave unlimited assets to your spouse tax-free, provided your spouse is a U.S. citizen. This marital deduction can be a cornerstone in planning to reduce estate taxes. Still, it's also essential to consider the eventual tax implications for your spouse's estate.

5. **Charitable Giving:** Donating to charity is not only a way to support causes you care about, but it can also reduce your estate tax liability. Bequests to charity are deductible from the value of your estate and can significantly lower the estate tax bill.

6. **Consider Lifetime Transfers:** Making transfers during your lifetime can be more tax-efficient than transferring wealth at death. This is because any appreciation on the assets after the transfer would occur outside of your estate, potentially leading to significant tax savings.

7. **Explore Business Succession Planning:** If you own a business, there are specific strategies, such as selling your interest to a family member at a reduced value or setting up a family-

limited partnership, that can help minimize taxes while ensuring a smooth transition of your business.

8. Keep Up with Tax Law Changes: Tax laws are constantly evolving, and strategies that are effective today may be less beneficial tomorrow. Staying informed about changes in tax legislation or working with a tax professional can help you adapt your estate plan to take advantage of new laws and avoid pitfalls.

Remember, each of these strategies comes with its own set of rules and limitations. It's crucial to work with an estate planning attorney and a tax advisor who can help tailor these strategies to your specific situation. By being proactive and informed, you can craft an estate plan that reflects your wishes and maximizes the financial benefits for your heirs.

State Estate and Inheritance Taxes

As we delve into estate planning, it's crucial to understand the federal tax implications and the state-specific nuances that can affect your estate. While the previous discussion focused on general strategies to minimize taxes, here we will navigate the often-overlooked terrain of state estate and inheritance taxes, which can significantly impact the legacy you leave behind.

Firstly, it's important to distinguish between estate taxes and inheritance taxes. The state levies estate taxes on the estate transfer before distribution to the beneficiaries. In contrast, inheritance taxes are imposed on the estate recipients after the assets have been distributed. Not all states impose these taxes, and those have varying rates and exemption thresholds.

For those states that impose estate taxes, the exemption amounts—below which no taxes are due—can vary widely. Some states align with the federal exemption amount, while others set their own, often much lower, thresholds. This means that even if your estate is not subject to federal estate taxes, it could still owe state estate taxes.

Inheritance taxes, on the other hand, are even less common. Still, they can surprise beneficiaries living in states that impose them. These taxes are usually based on the beneficiary's relationship to the decedent. Typically, spouses are exempt, and the rates may be lower for direct descendants. More distant relatives and non-relatives may find themselves facing higher tax rates.

Understanding the rules in your state is essential. Suppose you live in a state with estate or inheritance taxes or own property in such a state. In that case, it's wise to consult with a local estate planning attorney or tax advisor who can provide guidance tailored to your situation. They can help you explore strategies to minimize these state taxes, such as gifting during your lifetime or establishing trusts.

Moreover, if you're considering moving to another state, be aware that the estate and inheritance tax landscape should factor into your decision. A state with no estate or inheritance taxes might favor your estate planning goals more favorably.

Remember, estate planning is not a one-size-fits-all process. Each state's laws can significantly influence the effectiveness of your estate planning strategies. By staying informed and seeking professional advice, you can navigate these state-specific taxes and help ensure your estate is passed on according to your wishes with minimal tax burden on your heirs.

As we continue to explore the intricacies of estate planning, it's clear that life insurance can play a pivotal role in managing estate taxes. This versatile tool can provide liquidity to pay estate taxes and other expenses, ensuring your beneficiaries are not burdened with unexpected financial obligations. But before we delve into the strategic use of life insurance, it's essential to have a solid understanding of the state tax implications that might affect your estate.

The Role of Life Insurance in Estate Taxes

Life insurance is a powerful tool in estate planning, particularly when managing estate taxes. Its role is multifaceted, offering financial protection for your beneficiaries and strategic advantages for your estate's tax liabilities. Understanding how life insurance can be used to address estate taxes will help you make informed decisions as you structure your estate plan.

When you pass away, your estate may be subject to federal estate taxes if its value exceeds the exemption threshold the Internal Revenue Service (IRS) set. As of the time of writing, this threshold is in the millions of dollars, but it's essential to stay updated as tax laws and exemption limits can change. Suppose your estate is large enough to owe estate taxes. In that case, the proceeds from a life insurance policy can be a source of liquidity to pay these taxes without the need to sell off assets.

One of the key benefits of life insurance is that the death benefit paid out to beneficiaries is generally income tax-free. This means your loved ones can receive significant money without worrying about a tax bill on those funds. However, the value of the life insurance policy is included in your estate for estate tax purposes if you own the policy at the time of your death. This inclusion could push your estate over the exemption limit and result in a higher tax liability.

To avoid having the life insurance proceeds included in your estate, consider creating an irrevocable life insurance trust (ILIT). You relinquish control by transferring ownership of the life insurance policy to the ILIT. As a result, the proceeds are not considered part of your estate when you die. This means they won't be subject to estate taxes. The trust becomes the policy owner and beneficiary. Upon your death, the trust distributes the proceeds to your designated beneficiaries according to the terms you've set forth.

It's important to note that setting up an ILIT and transferring your life insurance policy into it must be done correctly to ensure that it achieves the desired tax benefits. There are specific rules and potential pitfalls to be aware of, such as the three-year rule, which states that if you die within three years of transferring the policy to the ILIT, the IRS will still consider the insurance proceeds as part of your estate. Therefore, planning and working with an experienced estate planning attorney is essential to navigate these complexities.

Additionally, life insurance can be used to provide for any potential liquidity needs your estate might have. For example, suppose your estate consists mainly of illiquid assets like real estate or a family business. In that case, your heirs might be challenged to obtain the cash needed to pay estate taxes. Life insurance proceeds can provide the necessary funds to cover these taxes without requiring your heirs to sell off assets, often at a hasty discount.

In summary, life insurance can play a pivotal role in estate planning by providing tax-free funds to beneficiaries, offering a means to pay estate taxes, and ensuring that your estate's assets are not unnecessarily liquidated to meet tax obligations. By considering the use of life insurance and an ILIT, you can create a more efficient and tax-effective estate plan. As with all aspects of estate planning, it's wise to consult professionals who can guide you through the process and help tailor a strategy to your specific needs and goals.

Chapter Summary

- Estate taxes or "death taxes" are levied on assets inherited after someone passes away, but only if the estate exceeds a specific exemption limit.
- The federal estate tax exemption is high, removing most estates from its reach. Still, the tax rate for eligible estates can be substantial.

- Some states have their own estate or inheritance taxes with different exemption levels and rates, which must be considered in estate planning.
- Gift taxes are imposed on property transferred during the giver's lifetime, with annual and lifetime exemptions to prevent avoidance of estate taxes.
- Strategic gifting within exemption limits can reduce the taxable estate size and lower the estate tax burden upon death.
- Utilizing the annual gift tax exclusion, paying for medical and educational expenses, setting up trusts, and charitable giving are strategies to minimize estate taxes.
- State estate and inheritance taxes vary, with different exemption amounts and rates, and should be factored into estate planning.
- Life insurance can provide liquidity to pay estate taxes and protect beneficiaries. Still, if owned by the deceased, it may increase estate tax liability unless placed in an irrevocable life insurance trust (ILIT).

5

HEALTHCARE DECISIONS AND ADVANCE DIRECTIVES

Healthcare Power of Attorney

Regarding estate planning, one of the most personal and significant decisions you can make is who will make healthcare decisions for you if you cannot do so yourself. This is where a Healthcare Power of Attorney (HPOA) becomes an essential part of your planning toolkit.

A Healthcare Power of Attorney is a legal document allowing you to appoint someone you trust, often called your agent or proxy, to make medical decisions on your behalf. If you are incapacitated, this person will have the authority to speak with your doctors, access your medical records, and make decisions about treatments, including life-sustaining measures.

Choosing your agent is a decision that should not be taken lightly. Someone who knows you well, understands your wishes, and is willing to advocate. It's also wise to select an alternate agent in case your primary choice is unable or unwilling to serve when the time comes.

When drafting a Healthcare Power of Attorney, being as transparent as possible about your preferences for medical care is essential. While it's impossible to anticipate every medical scenario, you can guide your general values and desires regarding quality of life, pain management, and any specific treatments you would or would not want.

One common misconception is that a Healthcare Power of Attorney is only for the elderly or those with chronic illnesses. However, unexpected medical situations can arise at any age, making it a prudent choice for any adult to have an HPOA in place.

After completing your Healthcare Power of Attorney, you must inform your chosen agent and discuss your wishes with them. You should also provide them with a copy of the document and inform your primary care physician and any specialists you see regularly. Keeping the document accessible, and perhaps even in an electronic format that can be easily shared, ensures that it can be quickly referenced when needed.

Remember, a Healthcare Power of Attorney can be revoked or changed if you are still competent. Life changes, such as marriage, divorce, or the death of your chosen agent, may necessitate a review and update of your HPOA. Regularly reviewing your estate planning documents ensures they reflect your current wishes and circumstances.

A Healthcare Power of Attorney is about maintaining control over your healthcare decisions, even when you cannot articulate them yourself. It's a powerful tool that provides peace of mind, knowing that your health and well-being will be in trusted hands if you cannot decide independently.

Living Wills and Medical Directives

In the realm of estate planning, preparing for the unexpected is a prudent step. While we've discussed the importance of designating someone to make healthcare decisions on your behalf through a healthcare power of attorney, it's equally crucial to delve into the specifics of your healthcare preferences. This is where living wills and medical directives come into play.

A living will is a written document that details your wishes regarding medical treatment in situations where you cannot communicate your decisions due to illness or incapacity. It's a proactive measure that provides clear instructions on what medical actions should be taken on your behalf. This can include your preferences on life-sustaining measures such as artificial hydration and nutrition, mechanical ventilation, or other forms of life support.

Creating a living will requires careful reflection on your values and beliefs about quality of life and end-of-life care. Discussing your wishes with family members and your healthcare provider is advisable to ensure they understand your preferences. Remember, living will become effective only under the specific conditions outlined in the document, typically when you are terminally ill or permanently unconscious with no expectation of recovery.

Medical directives, often used interchangeably with living wills, can also encompass other types of instructions, such as organ donation preferences and pain management. These directives provide a comprehensive guide to healthcare professionals and loved ones, ensuring that your healthcare treatment aligns with your wishes.

It's important to note that living wills and medical directives are legally binding documents, and their validity can vary from state to state. Therefore, ensuring that your documents comply with your state's laws is essential. Also, have them reviewed by an attorney specializing in estate planning to confirm that they accurately express your intentions.

Once you have prepared your living will and medical directives, it's crucial to keep them accessible. Inform your healthcare power of attorney, family members, and primary care physician of their existence and location. Some individuals carry a card in their wallet indicating the presence of a living will and where it can be found.

In summary, living wills and medical directives are critical components of a comprehensive estate plan. They provide peace of mind, knowing that your healthcare wishes will be respected even when you cannot voice them. By taking the time to create these documents, you are not only making decisions for yourself but also easing the burden on your loved ones during challenging times.

As we continue to navigate the intricacies of healthcare decisions within estate planning, we must consider all scenarios, including the potential need for a Do Not Resuscitate order, which we will explore in the following discussion.

Do Not Resuscitate Orders (DNR)

As we delve further into healthcare decisions within estate planning, it's essential to understand the role of do-not-resuscitate orders, commonly known as DNRs. These specific medical orders can be a critical component of your advance directives. While living wills and medical directives outline a range of preferences for care, a DNR is a more focused document that addresses a particular situation: whether or not you wish to receive cardiopulmonary resuscitation (CPR) if your heart stops beating or you stop breathing.

A DNR is not a decision to be taken lightly, as it can determine the course of action medical personnel will take in a life-threatening situation. It's essential to consider your values, beliefs, and what quality of life means to you when deciding whether to have a DNR in place. This decision should be made after careful discussion with your healthcare provider, understanding such an order's potential outcomes and implications.

If you choose to have a DNR, it's crucial to ensure that this order is readily accessible to healthcare providers. Unlike other estate planning documents that might be stored away, a DNR must be immediately available in an emergency. This might mean having a copy at home, in your wallet, or registered with a hospital or primary care physician. Some states even have registries for such orders to ensure emergency responders can access them quickly.

It's also worth noting that DNR orders are not one-size-fits-all. They can be tailored to your specific health situation and preferences. For example, some people may want a DNR in place only if they have a terminal illness. In contrast, others may want it to apply regardless of their health status. The nuances of your DNR can be discussed with your healthcare provider to ensure that it aligns with your wishes.

Remember, a DNR is a legally binding document that will guide medical professionals in an emergency. Therefore, reviewing and updating it as your health status or preferences change is imperative. Like all aspects of estate planning, your decisions should reflect your current circumstances and wishes.

A DNR is a significant piece of your healthcare directive puzzle. It's a declaration of your wishes regarding life-saving measures and requires thoughtful consideration. As you plan for the future, remember that these healthcare decisions are as much a part of your legacy as your financial or material assets. They speak to the care you wish to receive and the dignity with which you choose to face life's most challenging moments.

The Importance of Communicating Your Wishes

In the estate planning journey, one of the most compassionate steps you can take is to ensure that your healthcare wishes are communicated to your loved ones and healthcare providers. This is not just about having the documents in place but also about having the conversations that clarify your intentions.

Imagine a scenario where you cannot speak for yourself due to a medical condition. With clear instructions from you, your family may be able to guess what you want regarding medical treatment. This can lead to confusion, family disputes, and decisions that may align differently with your desires. To prevent this, it's essential to articulate your healthcare preferences through advance directives and communicate these wishes to those involved in your care.

Advance directives are legal documents that allow you to spell out your decisions about end-of-life care beforehand. They provide a way to communicate your wishes to family, friends, and healthcare professionals and to avoid confusion later on. These directives come in several forms, including living wills and durable powers of attorney for healthcare.

A living will is a written, legal document that spells out the types of medical treatments and life-sustaining measures you do and do not want. This could include your wishes regarding the use of dialysis, ventilation, resuscitation, tube feeding, and organ or tissue donation. On the other hand, a durable power of attorney for healthcare allows you to appoint someone you trust to make health decisions on your behalf if you cannot do so.

More than filling out these forms and tucking them away in a safe deposit box is required. It would help if you discussed your wishes in detail with the person or people designated to make decisions on your behalf. This can include family members, close friends, or a healthcare proxy. These conversations can be difficult, but they are crucial. They provide an opportunity to explain the values and experiences that have shaped your healthcare preferences. Moreover, they give your loved ones the clarity and confidence to make decisions that honor your wishes.

In addition to family and friends, your healthcare providers should also be informed of your advance directives. Ensure that copies of these documents are included in your medical records and that your primary care physician knows your preferences. This ensures that your wishes are known in an emergency and can be followed.

Remember, your healthcare wishes may evolve, so it's essential to review and update your advance directives periodically. Life changes such as a new diagnosis, the loss of a loved one, or changes in your personal beliefs can all influence your healthcare decisions.

Communicating your healthcare wishes is a continuous process, not a one-time event. It's about guiding those difficult decisions that may need to be made when you cannot make them yourself. By taking these steps, you can alleviate the burden on your loved ones and ensure that your healthcare preferences are respected, no matter what the future holds.

HIPAA Authorizations

In estate planning, understanding the role of HIPAA authorizations within the context of healthcare decisions is a critical component. HIPAA, which stands for the Health Insurance Portability and Accountability Act, is a federal law that, among other things, protects the privacy of an individual's health information. When planning for the future, it's important to consider who will have access to your medical records if you cannot communicate your wishes directly.

A HIPAA authorization is a legal document allowing individuals to receive information about their health status. This is separate from a healthcare power of attorney or an advance directive. However, they often work in conjunction with one another. While a healthcare power of attorney designates someone to make healthcare decisions on your behalf, a HIPAA authorization provides that person, or any other individuals you choose, with the necessary access to your medical information to make informed decisions.

Creating an HIPAA authorization involves specifying the individuals you wish to grant access to your medical records. This could be a spouse, adult children, other family members, or close friends. Trusting that the individuals you name will respect your privacy while also advocating for your health care preferences is essential.

When drafting a HIPAA authorization, you can define the scope of the information disclosed. You could allow full access to your medical records or limit it to certain types of information. Additionally, you can set an expiration date for the authorization or state that it remains in effect until you revoke it.

It's also worth noting that even your closest family members may be denied access to your medical information without HIPAA authorization. This can be particularly distressing in emergencies when timely knowledge of your medical history, allergies, or medications could influence the care you receive.

To ensure that your HIPAA authorization effectively serves its purpose, it's advisable to consult with an attorney who specializes in estate planning. They can help you navigate the complexities of the law and tailor the document to your specific needs. Once completed, copies of your HIPAA authorization should be given to your healthcare providers, the individuals you've authorized, and possibly your attorney.

Remember, a HIPAA authorization is a safeguard, ensuring that those you trust can access the information necessary to advocate for your care according to your wishes. It's a vital piece of the healthcare puzzle in estate planning, complementing other advance directives and ensuring a comprehensive approach to your future healthcare decisions.

Chapter Summary

- A Healthcare Power of Attorney (HPOA) allows you to appoint someone to make medical decisions if you're incapacitated.
- Choosing a trusted individual as your agent and clearly outlining your medical care preferences in the HPOA is essential.
- Living wills and medical directives specify your wishes for medical treatment and end-of-life care, including life-sustaining measures.
- Do Not Resuscitate Orders (DNRs) indicate whether you want CPR if your heart stops or you stop breathing.
- Clear communication of your healthcare wishes to loved ones and healthcare providers is crucial to prevent confusion and disputes.
- Advance directives, including living wills and durable powers of attorney for healthcare, should be discussed with those who may be involved in your care.
- HIPAA authorizations allow specified individuals to access your medical records to make informed decisions on your behalf.
- Regularly reviewing and updating all healthcare directives is essential to ensure they reflect your current wishes and circumstances.

6
PROTECTING YOUR ESTATE

Asset Protection Strategies

As we delve into asset protection strategies within estate planning, it's crucial to understand insurance's role in safeguarding your financial legacy. Insurance acts as a buffer against unforeseen events that could erode your estate's value or burden your heirs with unexpected liabilities.

One of the primary insurance measures that can be employed is life insurance. A well-structured life insurance policy can provide immediate liquidity to your estate upon passing. This infusion of cash can be instrumental in covering estate taxes, debts, and other obligations without requiring your heirs to hastily liquidate assets, which might otherwise be sold at an inopportune time or a loss. Moreover, life insurance proceeds are generally income tax-free to beneficiaries, which makes them an efficient tool for transferring wealth.

Another vital insurance strategy involves the use of disability insurance. While often overlooked, disability insurance is a cornerstone of a comprehensive estate plan. If you cannot work due to illness or injury, disability insurance can replace a portion of your income. This ensures that your financial needs are met without dipping into the savings and investments earmarked for your estate, thereby preserving the value you intend to pass on to your heirs.

Long-term care insurance is also a critical component of protecting your assets. The cost of long-term care, whether in-home care or a stay in a nursing facility, can be staggering and quickly deplete an estate. By securing long-term care insurance, you can shield your assets from these significant expenses, ensuring that your estate remains intact for your beneficiaries.

In addition to life, disability, and long-term care insurance, property and casualty insurance should not be neglected. This type of insurance protects against losses to your tangible assets, such as your home, automobiles, and personal property. Adequate coverage can prevent scenarios where your estate becomes liable for damages exceeding your policy limits, which could result in the need to liquidate assets to cover these costs.

Lastly, consider an umbrella liability policy. This form of insurance provides an extra layer of protection above and beyond the limits of your homeowners and auto insurance policies. In the event of a lawsuit, an umbrella policy can help protect your estate from being eroded by legal judgments or settlements that exceed standard policy limits.

Incorporating these insurance strategies into your estate plan is more than a one-size-fits-all proposition. It requires careful evaluation of your unique circumstances, including your assets, family structure, and long-term objectives. Consulting with insurance professionals and estate planning attorneys can help tailor these protective measures to fit your needs, ensuring your estate is well-defended against life's unexpected twists and turns.

By thoughtfully integrating insurance into your estate planning, you create a robust shield around the wealth you've worked so hard to accumulate. This provides peace of mind but also secures the financial well-being of your loved ones for the future.

Insurance as a Protective Measure

In the realm of estate planning, one of the most effective tools for safeguarding your financial legacy is insurance. While insurance is widely understood in the context of health or auto protection, its role in estate planning should be more appreciated. Yet, it is a critical component in a comprehensive plan to protect your assets and fulfill your wishes after passing.

Insurance can serve as a protective measure in several ways. Firstly, life insurance is a cornerstone of estate planning. It provides a death benefit to your beneficiaries, which can help cover living expenses, pay off debts, and maintain their standard of living when you are no longer there to provide for them. It can also be used to pay estate taxes, thus preserving the estate's value for your heirs. The key is to ensure that the amount of coverage is adequate to meet the needs of your beneficiaries and aligns with your overall estate plan.

Another aspect of insurance that is essential for estate protection is disability insurance. This coverage replaces income if you cannot work due to a disability. It ensures that you and your family can meet financial obligations and maintain your lifestyle without depleting your savings or investments, which are likely a part of your estate.

Long-term care insurance is another protective measure that can preserve your estate. The cost of long-term care, whether in-home care or a stay in a nursing facility, can be excessive and quickly erode your savings. With long-term care insurance, you can cover these costs without liquidating assets you intend to pass on to your heirs.

Annuities can also play a role in protecting your estate. Certain annuities can provide a steady stream of income for life, which can be particularly useful if you outlive your other retirement savings. They can also offer death benefits to your beneficiaries.

It's important to note that your insurance policies' ownership and beneficiary designations should be carefully considered as part of your estate plan. Incorrect designations can lead to unintended consequences, such as benefits being subject to probate or going to unintended recipients. Therefore, it's crucial to review these designations regularly and update them as necessary, especially after significant life events like marriage, divorce, or the birth of a child.

In summary, insurance is not just about managing risks during your lifetime; it's also about ensuring that your estate is protected and can provide for your loved ones according to your wishes after you're gone. By integrating insurance into your estate plan, you can create a safety net that preserves your legacy and provides peace of mind.

The Role of Liability Coverage

When it comes to safeguarding your estate, understanding the role of liability coverage is crucial. Liability coverage serves as a shield, protecting your assets from potential claims that could arise from various incidents. This type of insurance is not just about covering the costs of a lawsuit; it's about preserving the legacy you've worked so hard to build for your beneficiaries.

Imagine for a moment that you're found responsible for an accident that causes significant injury to another person. The legal and medical expenses could be substantial. Without adequate liability coverage, your estate could be at risk to cover these costs. This is where liability insurance steps in, providing a financial buffer that can help protect your estate's value.

There are different types of liability coverage to consider. Homeowner's insurance, for example, typically includes a certain amount of liability protection in case someone is injured on your property. Auto insurance policies also include liability coverage for accidents while operating your vehicle. However, these standard policies often have coverage limits that may need to be revised to protect your assets fully in case of a severe claim.

This is where umbrella insurance policies become particularly valuable. An umbrella policy provides additional liability coverage beyond the limits of your other policies. It kicks in when the liability on these other policies has been exhausted, offering an extra layer of security. This policy is a critical component of estate protection for individuals with significant assets, as it extends coverage to one asset and potentially all of your assets.

Moreover, liability coverage can also protect against the unforeseen and the unpredictable. For instance, if you volunteer on the board of a local non-profit and a lawsuit is brought against the organization, your assets could be at risk if you don't have the appropriate liability coverage.

When evaluating your need for liability coverage, consider the total value of your assets, including your home, investments, and any businesses you own. The more you have at stake, the more coverage you should consider to ensure your estate is not depleted by a single claim or lawsuit. It's also wise to review your coverage periodically, especially after significant life events like purchasing a new home, starting a business, or acquiring valuable assets.

In essence, liability coverage is not just about protecting your wealth today; it's about ensuring that your estate plan stands firm against potential threats tomorrow. By incorporating sufficient liability coverage into your estate plan, you're taking a proactive step to shield your assets and secure the financial future of your loved ones.

Homestead Protections

As we delve into homestead protections within estate planning, it's essential to understand that your home is not just a physical shelter but also a cornerstone of your financial security. Homestead protections are legal provisions designed to safeguard a person's home's value from certain creditors during financial distress or upon the homeowner's death.

At its core, a homestead exemption allows you to declare a portion of your home's value as exempt from certain types of creditors' claims. This means that, up to a specific value, your home cannot be forced into sale by the claims of unsecured creditors. However, it's important to note that this protection does not extend to secured creditors, such as mortgage lenders or those holding liens against the property.

The extent of homestead protections can vary significantly from one state to another. Some states offer generous exemptions that protect a large portion of the home's value if not all. Other states may provide more modest protections, and a few may have restrictions that make the exemptions applicable only to specific groups, such as older people or people with a disability.

You must typically file a declaration with the local county recorder's office to claim a homestead exemption. This declaration should state that the property in question is your primary residence and, thus, should be treated as a homestead. It's crucial to understand your state's specific process and requirements, as failing to properly declare your homestead can result in missing out on these valuable protections.

One of the critical benefits of homestead protections is that they can provide a sense of security for your family. In the event of your passing, the homestead exemption can help ensure that your loved ones have a place to live, as the exempted value of the home is often protected from claims against the estate.

Moreover, homestead protections can be particularly beneficial for those facing financial hardship. In the face of mounting debts, the knowledge that your home may be shielded from certain creditors can provide much-needed peace of mind and stability.

However, it's also essential to recognize the limitations of homestead exemptions. They do not protect against all types of debts. For example, they typically do not protect against tax liens, alimony, or child support obligations. Additionally, creditors could target excess equity if you have equity in your home that exceeds the exemption limit.

In summary, homestead protections are a critical component of estate planning that can offer significant benefits. They provide a layer of security for your most valuable asset—your home—ensuring that it remains a sanctuary for you and your family, even in uncertain times. To fully leverage these protections, it's essential to understand the specific laws in your state and to take the necessary steps to claim your homestead exemption. Consulting with a knowledgeable estate planning attorney can help you navigate these waters and make the most of the protections available.

Protecting Assets from Creditors

In estate planning, safeguarding your assets from creditors is critical to ensure that your hard-earned wealth is passed on to your loved ones rather than being depleted by legal claims. While homestead protections can offer a shield for your primary residence, there are additional strategies to consider for the broader scope of your estate.

One such strategy is the use of trust. Trusts can be a powerful tool in estate planning, serving multiple purposes, including creditor protection. By placing assets into a trust, you effectively remove ownership from your estate and place it under the control of a trustee. This separation can protect those assets from creditors, as the assets are no longer yours but a trust property. There are various types of trusts, such as irrevocable trusts, which, once established, cannot be altered or revoked by the grantor. This irrevocability is critical to the trust's ability to protect assets from creditors.

Another method to consider is the establishment of retirement accounts, like IRAs and 401(k)s, which often come with statutory protections. These accounts are typically legally recognized as exempt from creditors' claims up to certain limits. It's essential to understand the specific protections offered by your state, as they can vary significantly.

Life insurance policies and annuities can also play a role in protecting your assets. The cash value of life insurance policies and the payouts from annuities are often protected from creditors, depending on your state's laws. These financial products must be structured correctly to ensure they provide the intended protection, so it's advisable to consult a financial advisor or estate planning attorney to navigate these options.

Asset protection should be considered an integral part of your estate planning process. It's also worth noting that timing is crucial; asset protection strategies are most effective when implemented before any claims or liabilities arise. Once a claim is made or even anticipated, transferring assets to protect them from creditors could be considered a fraudulent conveyance.

Lastly, maintaining proper insurance coverage is a straightforward yet vital component of protecting your estate. Liability insurance, umbrella policies, and other forms of insurance can provide a first line of defense against claims, preserving your estate's assets for your intended beneficiaries.

Remember, the goal of asset protection is not to evade legitimate debts or responsibilities but to ensure that you have a plan in place that safeguards your estate for the future you envision for your family. As with all aspects of estate planning, it's wise to seek professional advice tailored to your specific situation to ensure that your asset protection strategy is effective and compliant with current laws and regulations.

Chapter Summary

- Insurance is a critical component of estate planning, providing a financial safety net for unforeseen events.
- Life insurance offers immediate liquidity for estate taxes and debts, and proceeds are typically tax-free to beneficiaries.
- Disability insurance replaces income in case of inability to work, preserving estate value for heirs.
- Long-term care insurance covers the high care costs without depleting estate assets.
- Property and casualty insurance protects tangible assets, and umbrella policies offer additional liability coverage.
- Insurance policies should be carefully aligned with estate plans, with correct ownership and beneficiary designations.
- Liability coverage, including umbrella policies, protects assets from legal claims and lawsuits.
- Homestead protections shield a primary residence from certain creditors, with varying levels of protection by the state.

7

THE ROLE OF EXECUTORS AND TRUSTEES

Duties of an Executor

When someone passes away, their estate must be settled. This involves managing and distributing their assets according to their will, if one exists, or according to state laws if they died intestate, meaning without a will. The person responsible for this task is known as the executor. If you're new to estate planning, understanding the duties of an executor is crucial, as they play a pivotal role in ensuring that your final wishes are carried out correctly.

The executor's role begins immediately after death. Their first duty is to locate and review the deceased's will to understand its instructions and wishes. This document outlines who will inherit the assets and may contain specific distribution directions.

Once the will is located, the executor must file it with the appropriate probate court. Probate is the legal process through which the deceased's assets are appropriately distributed. The executor is responsible for navigating this process, which includes proving the will's validity, if necessary.

After initiating probate, the executor must take inventory of the deceased's assets. This can be a complex task, especially if the deceased owned extensive property or had a variety of investments. The executor must be thorough, ensuring that all assets are accounted for, from real estate and vehicles to stocks, bonds, and personal belongings.

The executor is also responsible for managing the deceased's financial responsibilities. This includes paying any outstanding debts and taxes. They must ensure that the estate's bills, such as utilities, mortgages, and credit card debts, are paid from its funds. Additionally, they must file final income tax returns on behalf of the deceased.

Another critical duty of the executor is to maintain the property until it can be distributed or sold. This may involve securing a vacant home, managing investment accounts, or ensuring that a business continues to operate smoothly.

Once debts and taxes are settled, the executor can distribute the remaining assets to the beneficiaries as outlined in the will. This process must be done with care to ensure that each beneficiary receives what they are entitled to. Suppose there are any disputes among the beneficiaries. In that case, the executor must handle these diplomatically and by the will and the law.

Finally, the executor must provide an accounting of all transactions they've made on behalf of the estate. This includes all expenses paid, debts settled, and distributions to beneficiaries. This accounting is typically presented to the probate court and the beneficiaries.

Being an executor is a significant responsibility that requires organization, attention to detail, and a fair amount of time. It's a role that should not be taken lightly, as the executor is entrusted with ensuring that the deceased's wishes are honored and their beneficiaries are cared for. As we move forward, we'll discuss how to select someone capable and willing to take on this vital role.

Selecting an Executor

In the estate planning journey, one of the pivotal decisions you'll make is selecting an executor for your will. This individual will manage your estate after you pass away, ensuring that your wishes are honored and your assets are distributed according to your instructions. Given the role's gravity, approaching this choice carefully is essential.

When considering whom to appoint as your executor, you should look for someone trustworthy but also organized, communicative, and capable of handling financial matters. It's not just about choosing someone close to you; it's about selecting someone who can navigate estate administration's complexities.

Start by considering the scope of your estate and the complexity of the tasks at hand. If your estate is relatively straightforward, a family member or a close friend who is diligent and detail-oriented might be a suitable choice. However, consider someone with legal or financial expertise or a professional executor for more complex estates, such as a trust company.

It's also essential to think about the potential burden on the executor. Administering an estate can be time-consuming and emotionally taxing, especially if it involves selling property, managing investments, or dealing with family disputes. Ensure the person you choose is willing and able to take on these responsibilities.

Another critical factor is the location of your executor. Ideally, they should be near most of your assets to facilitate easier management and reduce travel time and expenses. However, with today's technology, distance can be less of a barrier, provided the executor is comfortable with digital communication and document handling.

Before finalizing your decision, have a candid conversation with your potential executor. Discuss your expectations, the extent of the duties, and whether they feel comfortable taking on the role. Transparency at this stage can prevent misunderstandings and ensure that your estate is in good hands.

Lastly, it's wise to name an alternate executor in your will. Life is unpredictable, and if your primary choice cannot serve due to unforeseen circumstances, having a backup ensures that your estate will still be managed as you intended.

Remember, the role of an executor is significant, and the person you choose will have a lasting impact on how your legacy is carried out. Take your time, weigh your options, and choose someone who embodies the diligence and integrity required to honor your final wishes.

Duties of a Trustee

In estate planning, understanding the role of a trustee is as crucial as selecting one. A trustee is someone you appoint to manage the trust you've created, and their responsibilities are both broad and specific, governed by the terms of the trust agreement and state law. Let's delve into what it means to be a trustee and the duties of this vital role.

Firstly, a trustee must adhere to the trust's terms. This is the trustee's legal and moral compass. The trust document is like a roadmap; the trustee is the navigator, ensuring the trust's assets are managed and distributed according to the grantor's wishes. This means reading and understanding the document thoroughly, seeking legal advice, and executing the terms faithfully.

A trustee is also responsible for managing the trust's assets. This involves a prudent investment strategy that balances growth with risk, always considering the beneficiaries' best interests. The trustee must avoid speculative investments and ensure the trust's assets are productive. If the trust holds real estate, the trustee must maintain the property, collect rent, and pay expenses. The trustee must monitor performance and adjust if it holds financial assets.

Another critical duty is to maintain clear, accurate, and detailed records. This includes all income and expenses related to the trust, investments, distributions, and other financial transactions. These records are vital for tax purposes and reporting to beneficiaries entitled to information about the trust's administration.

Speaking of beneficiaries, the trustee must communicate with them regularly, providing updates on the trust's assets and the trustee's actions. This fosters transparency and trust, and it also helps to prevent misunderstandings or disputes.

The trustee also must file taxes for the trust. Trusts are subject to their own tax rules, and the trustee must ensure that all federal and state tax returns are filed on time and that any taxes due are paid from the trust's assets.

Lastly, the trustee must be fair and impartial to all beneficiaries. This can be challenging, especially if the beneficiaries have conflicting interests or if the trustee has a personal relationship with them. The trustee must navigate these relationships carefully, always acting reasonably and in line with the trust's terms.

Being a trustee is a significant responsibility, requiring diligence, fairness, and a commitment to acting in the best interests of the beneficiaries. It's not a role to be taken lightly, and it's essential for anyone creating a trust to choose their trustee wisely.

With the right person in place, trust can be a powerful tool for managing and protecting assets for the benefit of loved ones.

Selecting a Trustee

After understanding the responsibilities that come with the role of a trustee, as outlined in the previous section, you're now faced with the crucial decision of selecting the right individual or institution to manage your trust. This decision is not to be taken lightly, as the trustee will have significant control over your assets and the welfare of your beneficiaries after you're gone.

When choosing a trustee, consider the following attributes and qualifications to ensure that your estate is in good hands:

- **Trustworthiness:** Above all, the trustee must be someone you can trust implicitly. This person will manage your assets and make decisions that affect your beneficiaries' financial future. Look for someone with a solid moral compass who has demonstrated reliability and integrity in their personal and professional life.
- **Financial Acumen:** The trustee should understand financial matters, investments, and the legal responsibilities of trust management. Professionals can always be consulted and don't need to be a financial expert. Still, a solid grasp of financial concepts is essential.
- **Organizational Skills:** Managing trust requires much organization. The trustee must keep accurate records, file taxes for the trust, and communicate effectively with beneficiaries. Someone who is detail-oriented and has strong administrative skills would be a good fit for this role.
- **Impartiality:** It's essential that the trustee can act impartially and in the best interest of all beneficiaries.

This can be challenging if the trustee is also a beneficiary or has a close relationship with one. Sometimes, appointing an independent third party, such as a trust company or a professional trustee, can help ensure that decisions are made without bias.
- **Availability:** Serving as a trustee is not a one-time task; it's an ongoing responsibility that can last many years. Make sure the person you choose has the time and willingness to commit to managing the trust for as long as necessary.
- **Willingness to Serve:** Never assume someone is willing to take on the role of trustee. Have a candid conversation with your potential trustee to ensure they understand the duties involved and are willing to accept the responsibility.
- **Age and Health:** Consider the age and health of your potential trustee. Choosing someone likely to predecease you or become incapacitated could lead to complications. It's also wise to name a successor trustee who can step in if your first choice cannot fulfill their duties.

Sometimes, you may find that no individual in your circle meets all these criteria, or you may prefer to avoid burdening friends or family with the responsibility. In such instances, you can opt for a professional trustee like a bank or trust company. These entities have the expertise and resources to manage trusts effectively but charge fees for their services.

Remember, the trustee you select will be pivotal in carrying out your wishes and managing your legacy. Take your time, weigh your options, and choose someone who will honor your trust and act in the best interests of your beneficiaries. Once you have selected, the next step will be to ensure that your estate and trust administration is set up for smooth management, which we will explore further.

Managing Estate and Trust Administration

Having selected a trustee, it's essential to understand the practical side of what happens next. The administration of an estate or trust is a critical phase where the decisions of the executor or trustee come to life, impacting beneficiaries and the legacy of the deceased. As you embark on this journey, you'll find that managing an estate or trust is akin to steering a ship through a series of checkpoints, each with its rules and potential challenges.

Firstly, the executor or trustee must take inventory of the estate's assets. This includes everything from bank accounts, real estate, stocks, and bonds to personal items like jewelry and artwork. It's a meticulous process that requires attention to detail and, often, detective work. The goal is to establish a clear picture of what the estate comprises, which will be crucial for the next steps.

Once the inventory is complete, the executor or trustee secures these assets. This might involve changing locks on the property, updating account information, and ensuring that all assets are safe from theft or damage. It's a role that requires high responsibility and trustworthiness, as you're safeguarding someone's lifetime of hard work and investment.

The next task is to settle any debts and liabilities. Before beneficiaries receive their inheritance, the executor or trustee must pay all the deceased's outstanding debts. This might include final income taxes, personal loans, or credit card debts. It's essential to handle these obligations promptly and accurately to avoid any legal complications down the line.

After debts have been settled, the executor or trustee must manage the distribution of the estate according to the will or trust document. This is where your role becomes deeply personal, fulfilling the deceased's final wishes. It's a process that requires sensitivity and diplomacy, especially if multiple beneficiaries have different interests.

The executor or trustee must maintain clear and open communication with the beneficiaries throughout this process. They have a right to understand how the estate is being managed and when they can expect to receive their inheritance. Regular updates can help to build trust and reduce anxiety or conflict among the beneficiaries.

Finally, the executor or trustee must prepare and file all necessary tax returns for the estate. This can be a complex task, requiring a good understanding of tax laws and, often, the assistance of a professional accountant or tax advisor.

In summary, managing estate and trust administration is a multifaceted role that requires organizational skills, financial understanding, and a compassionate touch. It's about more than just numbers and legal documents; it's about honoring the wishes of someone who has placed their ultimate trust in you. As you navigate this process, remember that your role is both a privilege and a responsibility, and your actions will leave a lasting impact on the lives the estate touches.

Chapter Summary

- Executors are responsible for settling an estate, including managing and distributing assets according to the will or state laws if there is no will.
- Executors must locate the will, fill it with the probate court, inventory assets, manage financial responsibilities, and maintain the property until distribution.
- They must pay the deceased's debts and taxes, distribute assets to beneficiaries, handle disputes, and provide an accounting of all transactions.
- Selecting an executor requires considering trustworthiness, organizational skills, financial

understanding, willingness to serve, and naming an alternate.
- Trustees manage trusts according to the trust document and state law, balancing growth with investment risk and maintaining clear records.
- Trustees must communicate with beneficiaries, file trust taxes, and act impartially and fairly to all beneficiaries.
- When selecting a trustee, consider trustworthiness, financial knowledge, organizational skills, impartiality, availability, willingness to serve, and age and health.
- Estate and trust administration involves inventorying assets, securing them, settling debts, distributing inheritance, communicating with beneficiaries, and filing tax returns.

8

PLANNING FOR INCAPACITY

Financial Power of Attorney

When considering the future and the unexpected twists it may hold, it's crucial to prepare not just for the distribution of your assets after you pass away but also for the possibility that you might one day be unable to manage your financial affairs due to incapacity. This is where a Financial Power of Attorney (POA) becomes essential in your estate planning toolkit.

A Financial Power of Attorney is a legal document that allows you to appoint someone you trust, often referred to as your "agent" or "attorney-in-fact," to manage your financial matters if you become incapacitated and unable to do so yourself. This person will have the authority to handle tasks such as paying your bills, managing your investments, and making other financial decisions on your behalf.

One of the primary benefits of having a Financial Power of Attorney in place is that it provides a clear directive and immediate authority to your chosen agent without needing court intervention. This can be exceptionally comforting, as it ensures that your financial matters will be handled according to your wishes by someone you have personally selected.

When drafting a Financial Power of Attorney, you have the flexibility to define the scope of your agent's powers. You can grant them broad authority to handle your financial affairs or limit their powers to specific tasks, accounts, or assets. Additionally, you can decide whether this power becomes effective immediately or only activates upon your incapacity, which a medical professional's evaluation can determine.

It's essential to choose an agent who is trustworthy and capable of managing financial matters prudently. This person should understand your values and wishes regarding your finances and be willing to act in your best interest. It's also wise to name a successor agent who can step in if your first choice is unable or unwilling to serve when the time comes.

Creating a Financial Power of Attorney requires careful consideration and, often, the guidance of a legal professional to ensure that the document is valid and reflects your intentions. Remember, the POA is revocable; you can change or cancel it anytime if you are mentally competent.

Without a Financial Power of Attorney, or if additional support is needed, the court may appoint a conservator to oversee an incapacitated person's financial affairs. This process, known as conservatorship, can be lengthy, costly, and more restrictive, so having a POA is generally preferable for many individuals planning for potential incapacity.

The Role of Conservatorships

In the estate planning journey, we've explored the importance of designating a financial power of attorney—a trusted individual who can manage your financial affairs should you become unable to do so yourself. However, there may be circumstances where a power of attorney is not in place or a situation arises that falls outside the scope of this document. In such cases, the court may appoint a conservator to step in. Let's delve into the role of conservatorships and how they function as a safety net in estate planning.

A conservatorship is a legal relationship established by a court order, where a person or organization, known as the conservator, is appointed to manage the financial and personal affairs of an adult deemed incapable of doing so themselves due to physical or mental limitations. This legal arrangement is particularly relevant when an individual has not made prior arrangements for incapacity or when disputes arise regarding the designated power of attorney.

Establishing a conservatorship can be initiated by a family member, a close friend, or any interested party concerned about the individual's well-being. The court then evaluates the evidence, which often includes medical testimony, to determine whether the person in question, often referred to as the conservatee, cannot handle their affairs.

Once a conservator is appointed, they are granted the authority to make decisions on behalf of the conservatee. These decisions can range from handling financial transactions, managing investments, paying bills, and selling property to making choices about living arrangements, health care, and other personal matters if a separate conservator of the person is appointed.

It's important to note that conservatorships have a significant level of court oversight. Conservators must provide regular reports and account for their actions to ensure that they act in the conservatee's best interests. This oversight is designed to protect the conservatee from potential abuse or neglect.

While conservatorships can offer a vital safety net, they can also be restrictive. They may involve a loss of autonomy for the conservatee. For this reason, many individuals prefer to plan by creating durable powers of attorney and health care directives, which allow them to choose who will make decisions for them in the event of incapacity.

In the digital age, our lives are increasingly intertwined with technology, which brings us to another aspect of estate planning: managing your digital legacy. As we move forward, we'll explore how to ensure that your online presence is handled according to your wishes, just as carefully as your offline assets.

Managing Your Digital Legacy

In the digital age, our lives are increasingly intertwined with technology, creating a substantial online presence that can outlive us. This digital footprint, comprising emails, social media accounts, online banking, and even virtual assets like domain names or cryptocurrency, constitutes what is known as your digital legacy. As part of planning for incapacity, managing this aspect of your estate is crucial to ensure your digital life is handled according to your wishes should you become unable to do so yourself.

Firstly, take inventory of your digital assets. This includes listing all your online accounts, such as email, social media, financial, shopping, and any websites you own. For each, note down the login credentials and how you would like each account handled. Some platforms have protocols for deceased or incapacitated users, so it's worth investigating and incorporating them into your plan.

Next, consider appointing a digital executor. This is someone you trust to manage your digital assets in line with your instructions. This role can be part of a broader power of attorney, or you can designate a separate digital power of attorney specifically for your online content. Ensure this person is tech-savvy and understands the sensitivity and confidentiality required to handle your digital legacy.

It's also essential to understand the legal landscape. The Revised Uniform Fiduciary Access to Digital Assets Act (RUFADAA), adopted by most states, allows you to give legal authority to your designated representative to access your digital assets. However, this requires explicit consent through estate planning documents, so include such permissions in your will, trust, or power of attorney.

Lastly, provide clear instructions for managing or disposing of your digital assets. This might include deleting certain accounts, archiving digital photos, or transferring valuable assets to beneficiaries. Be as specific as possible to avoid ambiguity leading to disputes or confusion.

Remember, managing your digital legacy is an ongoing process. You must update your estate plan accordingly as you acquire new digital assets or as online services change their policies. By taking these steps, you can ensure that your digital life is as well-organized and respectfully handled as the rest of your estate when you can no longer manage it yourself.

Chapter Summary

- A Financial Power of Attorney (POA) allows you to appoint someone to manage your finances if you become incapacitated.

- The appointed agent can handle tasks like paying bills and managing investments with immediate authority without court intervention.
- You can define the scope of the agent's powers and decide when the POA becomes effective immediately or upon incapacity.
- It's essential to choose a trustworthy and financially savvy agent and to consider naming a successor agent.
- A POA is revocable and can be changed if you are mentally competent.
- Without a POA, a court may appoint a conservator to manage your affairs, which can be a lengthy and costly process.
- Conservatorships involve court oversight and can be restrictive. Still, they serve as a safety net when no POA exists.

9

ESTATE PLANNING FOR BUSINESS OWNERS

Assessing Your Business Assets

As a business owner, your company is likely one of your most significant assets, and its value can substantially impact your estate. Assessing your business assets is a critical step in estate planning and requires a thorough and strategic approach. Let's delve into how to effectively evaluate your business holdings to ensure they align with your long-term estate planning goals.

Firstly, you'll need to determine the fair market value of your business. This can be a complex process, often requiring the expertise of a professional business appraiser. They will consider various factors, including your company's financial history, market position, and future earning potential. It's essential to have an accurate valuation, as this will influence your estate planning decisions, such as how to distribute shares among heirs or whether to sell the business.

Next, take stock of your business's tangible and intangible assets. Tangible assets include physical items like property, equipment, and inventory, while intangible assets include patents, trademarks, and goodwill. Understanding the full scope of what your business owns is essential for creating a comprehensive estate plan.

It would help if you also considered your business's liabilities. Debts and other financial obligations must be addressed in your estate plan to ensure they don't burden your heirs. Knowing the extent of these liabilities will help you make informed decisions about life insurance, asset distribution, and other estate planning tools.

Moreover, if your business has multiple owners, you'll need to review any existing agreements that may affect the transfer of your interests. These agreements can dictate what happens to your share of the business upon your death, and they should be aligned with your personal estate planning objectives.

Lastly, it's crucial to keep your business assessment up-to-date. Regularly revisiting and revising your valuation and asset inventory will help you adapt to market and business changes, ensuring your estate plan remains relevant and practical.

By thoroughly assessing your business assets, you lay the groundwork for the next steps in your estate planning journey. This careful evaluation will clarify your plans and offer peace of mind, knowing that your business legacy is well-prepared for the transition to the next generation.

Buy-Sell Agreements

As a business owner, creating a buy-sell agreement is one of the most critical components of your estate planning. This legally binding document outlines what happens to your share of the business in case of your death, disability, retirement, or if you decide to leave the company. It's a contingency plan that protects not only your interests but also those of your business partners and your family.

A buy-sell agreement can be compared to a prenuptial agreement for your business. It sets the terms for a buyout, ensuring that the remaining business owners have the right or the obligation to buy the departing owner's share at a predetermined price and under specific conditions. This agreement is crucial because it provides a clear path for the business to continue and can prevent potential disputes among remaining owners or between owners and the departing owner's heirs.

There are several types of buy-sell agreements, and the one you choose will depend on the nature of your business and your specific needs:

- **Cross-Purchase Agreements:** This type is used when there are few co-owners. Each owner buys a life insurance policy for the other owners. In death, the surviving owners use the insurance proceeds to buy the deceased owner's share of the business.
- **Entity-Purchase Agreements:** Also known as a stock redemption plan, the company purchases the departing owner's share. The business will own each owner's insurance policy and is responsible for the buyout.

- **Hybrid Agreements:** A combination of the two above allows the company and the individual co-owners to share the responsibility of buying out a departing owner's interest.

When drafting a buy-sell agreement, it's essential to consider how the buyout will be funded. Life and disability insurance are standard methods because they provide a funding source exactly when needed. However, the agreement might also include provisions for installment payments or other methods of financing the buyout.

Valuation of the business interest is another critical component of the buy-sell agreement. You'll need to decide how to determine the value of a business owner's interest. This could be a fixed price agreed upon by all owners, a formula based on the company's earnings or book value, or a process involving a professional business valuation during the buyout.

It's also essential to review and update your buy-sell agreement regularly. As your business grows and changes, the terms that made sense at one point may no longer be relevant or fair. Regular reviews, ideally with the assistance of a legal and financial advisor, ensure that the agreement continues to reflect the current state of the business and the wishes of all parties involved.

In conclusion, a well-structured buy-sell agreement is a cornerstone of business continuity planning. It provides a roadmap for the future of your business in the face of unforeseen events and helps ensure that your legacy endures. As you move forward with your estate planning, remember that the decisions you make today will shape the future of your business long after you're gone. With thoughtful planning and clear communication, you can create a lasting impact that benefits your family, business partners, and the enterprise you've worked hard to build.

Succession Planning

As a business owner, you've likely invested significant time, energy, and resources into building a successful enterprise. But what happens to your business when you can no longer lead it? This is where succession planning is an essential component of estate planning for business owners.

Succession planning is identifying and preparing new leaders to take over your business when you retire, become incapacitated, or pass away. It's about ensuring the continuity of your business and preserving the legacy you've worked so hard to create. With a clear succession plan, your business could avoid an uncertain future, which could affect not only your family's wealth but also the livelihood of your employees and the satisfaction of your customers.

To begin with, consider who is best suited to take over your business. This could be a family member, a trusted employee, or even an external candidate. Choosing someone with the right skills and vision is essential to keep the business thriving. Once you've identified potential successors, involve them early in the business, allowing them to gain the necessary experience and knowledge.

Next, you'll want to formalize the succession plan. This involves setting a timeline for the transition, defining the roles and responsibilities of the successor, and outlining the training process. It's also crucial to consider how ownership will be transferred. Will it be a gradual transfer of shares, a sale, or perhaps a gift as part of your estate?

Legal documentation is a crucial aspect of succession planning. Work with an attorney to draft a will, power of attorney, and other necessary legal documents supporting your succession plan. These documents will help ensure that your wishes are fulfilled and that the leadership transition happens smoothly.

Communication is another vital element of a successful succession plan. Communicating your plans to your family, your business's potential successor, and critical stakeholders is essential. Open and honest communication can prevent misunderstandings and conflicts that could jeopardize the future of your business.

Finally, review and update your succession plan regularly. As your business grows and changes, so too might your choice of successor or the transition structure. Regular reviews ensure that your plan remains relevant and practical.

In summary, succession planning is a proactive approach to safeguarding the future of your business. It's about making thoughtful decisions today to protect your business's value and ensure its success tomorrow. With a solid succession plan, you can rest assured that your business legacy will endure, providing peace of mind for you, your family, and all those connected to your enterprise.

Insurance for Business Owners

As a business owner, you've likely invested significant time, energy, and resources into building your enterprise. It's not just a source of income; it's a part of your legacy. That's why insurance plays a crucial role in estate planning for business owners. It serves as a safety net, ensuring that your business can continue to operate and support your loved ones even in your absence.

Let's start by discussing the types of insurance that are particularly important for business owners:

- **Life Insurance:** The cornerstone of any business owner's insurance strategy. A life insurance policy can provide the funds necessary to keep the business afloat during the transition period following your passing. The payout can help cover debts, pay for ongoing expenses, or fund a buy-sell agreement, which we'll touch on shortly.

- **Disability Insurance:** What if an illness or injury prevents you from running your business long before you pass away? Disability insurance can replace a portion of your lost income, helping maintain your living standard and keeping the business operational.
- **Key Person Insurance:** Your business may rely on one or a few individuals whose expertise and management are critical to its success. Key person insurance compensates the business if one of these vital individuals passes away or becomes incapacitated, providing the financial breathing room to find a replacement or restructure the company.
- **Buy-Sell Agreements Funded by Life Insurance:** A buy-sell agreement is a legally binding document that outlines what happens to a business when one of the owners dies or wishes to leave the company. Life insurance policies can be structured to fund these agreements, ensuring that there's capital available for the remaining owners to buy the departing owner's share without financial strain.
- **Property and Casualty Insurance:** While not directly related to your death or disability, property and casualty insurance protects the physical assets of your business from unforeseen events like fires, theft, or natural disasters. This type of insurance helps preserve your business's value for your heirs.
- **Liability Insurance:** This insurance protects your estate from claims that could arise from the operations of your business. Maintaining adequate coverage to shield your assets and those of your estate from potential lawsuits is essential.

When selecting insurance policies, consider the following:

- **The Value of Your Business:** How much is your business worth, and how much insurance will be needed to cover its value? This is a complex calculation that often requires the assistance of a professional appraiser or accountant.
- **Your Succession Plan:** Your insurance must tie directly into your succession plan. Who will take over the business? Will it be sold? The answers to these questions will influence the type and amount of insurance you should carry.
- **The Structure of Your Business:** Are you a sole proprietor, or do you have partners? The structure of your business will affect the kind of insurance policies you'll need.
- **Your Personal and Business Debts:** Insurance can help ensure that any debts you've guaranteed won't burden your family or business.

In conclusion, insurance for business owners is not just about protecting your interests; it's about safeguarding the future of your business and the financial security of your family and employees. By carefully selecting the suitable types and amounts of insurance, you can create a robust estate plan that addresses the unique challenges of business ownership. Remember, the goal is to provide peace of mind for yourself and your loved ones, knowing that the business you've worked so hard to build is protected against life's uncertainties.

Transferring Ownership and Control

As a business owner, you've invested significant time, energy, and resources into building your enterprise. It's not just a business but part of your legacy. That's why transferring ownership and control is a critical component of estate planning for business owners. This process ensures your business thrives and supports your beneficiaries according to your wishes after you leave.

When considering the transfer of your business, starting with a clear succession plan is essential. This plan outlines who will take over the business: family members, a partner, key employees, or an outside buyer. It also details the conditions under which the transfer will occur, such as retirement, disability, or death.

One common strategy for transferring ownership is through a buy-sell agreement. This legally binding contract stipulates how a partner's share of the business may be reassigned if that partner dies or leaves the company. The agreement can be funded with life insurance policies to ensure sufficient funds are available to buy out the departing partner's interest, allowing for a smoother transition and financial stability for the business.

Another option is to gift the business to your heirs during your lifetime. This can be done gradually to minimize taxes and to allow you to maintain some control as your successors become more involved in business operations. Be mindful, however, of the gift tax implications and the annual exclusion limits.

For those wishing to keep the business in the family, a family limited partnership (FLP) or a family limited liability company (FLLC) can be helpful. These structures allow you to transfer business shares to family members over time, often at a reduced tax cost, while retaining control over the business's direction.

Suppose you're considering selling the business outright. In that case, it's crucial to have a professional valuation done to determine a fair market price. This valuation will be important not only for a potential sale but also for estate tax purposes. It's also wise to consult a financial advisor to understand how the sale will impact your retirement and estate planning goals.

Lastly, it's essential to consider the potential impact of estate taxes on your business. With proper planning, strategies such as trusts, charitable contributions, and other tax planning techniques can minimize the estate tax burden and ensure that your heirs are not forced to sell the business to cover tax liabilities.

Remember, transferring ownership and control of your business is not a one-size-fits-all process. It requires careful planning, consideration of all stakeholders, and, often, the guidance of legal and financial professionals. By taking the time to establish a comprehensive plan, you can help secure the future of your business and provide for your heirs in the manner you envision.

Chapter Summary

- Determine your business's fair market value with a professional appraiser's help.
- Inventory your business's tangible and intangible assets to create a comprehensive estate plan.
- Address business liabilities in your estate plan to prevent them from burdening your heirs.
- Review any existing agreements with co-owners that may affect the transfer of business interests.
- Keep your business assessment current to ensure your estate plan adapts to changes in the market and business.
- Establish a buy-sell agreement to dictate what happens to your share of the business upon death or departure.
- Succession planning is crucial for identifying and preparing new leaders to take over the business.
- Select appropriate types and amounts of insurance to protect the business and support your loved ones after you're gone.

10

KEEPING YOUR ESTATE PLAN CURRENT

When to Review Your Estate Plan

Creating an estate plan is akin to capturing a snapshot of your life at a particular moment. As time marches on, your life and your estate plan evolve. It's not a 'set it and forget it' affair. Regular reviews ensure your estate plan accurately reflects your current wishes and circumstances. But when exactly should you dust off your estate documents and give them a thorough look-over?

Firstly, it's wise to mark your calendar for a biennial review. Every two years, take the time to sit down with your estate planning documents and go through them with a fine-tooth comb. This regular check-up will help you catch any changes in tax laws, estate laws, or personal preferences since your last review.

However, life only sometimes adheres to a schedule, and certain events can necessitate an immediate review of your estate plan. Significant life changes are the most apparent triggers for a review. These can include a marriage or divorce, which alters your relationship status and significantly impacts your estate planning decisions and beneficiary designations. The birth or adoption of a child is another joyous occasion that should prompt you to update your estate plan to include provisions for your new family member.

Similarly, the death of a loved one, mainly if they were included in your estate plan as a beneficiary or executor, requires immediate attention to adjust your plan accordingly. A significant change in your financial situation, such as receiving a large inheritance, winning the lottery, or suffering a substantial financial loss, also warrants a fresh look at your estate plan to ensure it still serves your best interests.

Additionally, you've moved to a different state. In that case, it's crucial to review your estate plan to ensure it complies with the laws of your new home. State laws regarding estate taxes, probate, and other estate planning issues can vary widely, and what was valid in one state may not be in another.

Another reason to review your estate plan is a change in your health or that of a family member. Suppose you or a loved one has been diagnosed with a severe illness or disability. In that case, you may need to make adjustments to your estate plan to address long-term care needs, medical directives, or the management of your affairs should you become incapacitated.

Finally, if there have been changes in the laws that affect estate planning—such as tax law reforms—it's essential to understand how these changes might affect your estate and whether any adjustments are needed to optimize your plan.

Remember, keeping your estate plan current is not just about adjusting to the adverse or unforeseen events in life. It's also about capturing the positive changes and ensuring that your plan reflects your life's journey accurately. Regular reviews and updates after significant life events will help ensure that your estate plan reflects your wishes and provide peace of mind that your legacy will be handled as you intended.

Life Events that Affect Your Estate Plan

As we navigate through life's journey, our circumstances inevitably change. These shifts, both big and small, can significantly impact the relevance and effectiveness of your estate plan. Understanding which life events can trigger a need for updates is crucial for ensuring that your wishes are honored and your loved ones are protected. Let's explore some of these pivotal moments and how they intertwine with your estate planning efforts.

Firstly, marriage is a joyful event that significantly changes one's life. If you've recently tied the knot, it's essential to reflect this in your estate plan. Consider including your spouse in your will, designate them as beneficiaries on retirement accounts, or grant them powers of attorney. Conversely, divorce is a life event requiring a thorough review of your estate plan. Removing your former spouse from any roles they previously held in your will, trusts, or as a beneficiary is a step that should be considered.

The arrival of children or grandchildren is another momentous occasion that should prompt a review of your estate plan. You may need to appoint guardians for minor children, set up trusts to manage their inheritance or make provisions for their education and care. As children grow and their circumstances change, your estate plan should evolve to reflect these developments.

Significant changes in your financial situation also warrant a review of your estate plan. This could include receiving a large inheritance, experiencing a substantial increase or decrease in the value of your assets, or starting a business. These financial shifts can affect how you wish to distribute your assets and may introduce new considerations for tax planning.

Health is another critical factor that can influence your estate plan. A diagnosis of a severe illness or a disability might lead to adjustments in your healthcare directives or living will. It's essential to ensure that your wishes regarding medical treatment and end-of-life care are clearly documented and that the individuals you've designated to make decisions on your behalf are still the right choices.

Lastly, relocation to a different state or country can affect your estate plan due to varying laws and regulations. It's advisable to consult with an estate planning attorney in your new location to ensure your plan complies with local laws and continues to serve your interests.

Each life event is a call to action—a reminder to revisit and potentially revise your estate plan. By keeping your plan aligned with your current circumstances, you can rest assured that your intentions will be honored and your loved ones will be cared for according to your wishes. Remember, an estate plan is not a static document but a dynamic framework that should adapt as your life unfolds.

Updating Beneficiaries

As we navigate through the journey of life, our relationships and circumstances evolve, often in ways we couldn't have anticipated when we first drafted our estate plans. It's crucial to remember that your estate plan is a living document, one that should grow and change as you do. A key component of keeping your estate plan current is regularly updating your beneficiaries.

Beneficiaries are the individuals or entities you designate to receive your assets upon passing. These can include family members, friends, charitable organizations, or trusts. Your beneficiary designations are found in various documents, such as wills, life insurance policies, retirement accounts, and investment portfolios.

Why is updating beneficiaries so important? Life events such as marriages, divorces, births, and deaths can drastically alter your original intentions for your estate. For instance, if you've named your spouse as a primary beneficiary and later divorced, you may not want your ex-spouse to remain the recipient of your assets. Similarly, the joyous arrival of children or grandchildren might prompt you to include them in your estate plan.

To update your beneficiaries, you'll need to review all documents where they are named. Start with your will and trust, if you have one, and then move on to your life insurance policies and retirement accounts like IRAs and 401(k)s. For each account or policy, you'll typically need to request a change of beneficiary form from the financial institution or insurance company. Fill out these forms with the new beneficiary information and submit them according to the provider's instructions.

It's also wise to consider contingent beneficiaries who will inherit if your primary beneficiary cannot do so. This adds an extra layer of protection and ensures that your assets are distributed according to your wishes, even if unexpected circumstances arise.

Remember, beneficiary designations often supersede instructions in your will. This means that even if your will states something different, the assets in accounts with a named beneficiary will go directly to that beneficiary. Therefore, ensuring that all designations are consistent with your overall estate plan is imperative.

As you update your beneficiaries, it's also an excellent time to reflect on the overall distribution of your assets. Are you dividing your estate in a way that aligns with your values and goals? Are there charitable causes you'd like to support? These considerations can guide you in making thoughtful and meaningful updates to your beneficiary designations.

In conclusion, keeping your beneficiaries up-to-date is vital to maintaining an effective estate plan. It's a task that requires attention to detail and an understanding of how various life changes impact your ultimate wishes for your legacy. By regularly reviewing and revising your beneficiary designations, you can rest assured that your assets will be distributed according to your current intentions, providing peace of mind for you and your loved ones.

Revising Legal Documents

As you've taken the critical step of designating beneficiaries, which we've discussed earlier, it's equally crucial to ensure that all your legal documents within your estate plan are up-to-date. Life is ever-changing, and your estate plan should be a living document that reflects your current circumstances and wishes. Let's delve into the how and why of revising legal documents as part of keeping your estate plan current.

Firstly, it's essential to understand which documents need revising. The core legal documents in most estate plans include your will, trust agreements, powers of attorney, and healthcare directives. Each serves a distinct purpose and may need to be updated for different reasons.

Your will, for instance, outlines how you want your assets distributed and who will care for any minor children. Significant life events such as marriage, divorce, the birth of a child, or the death of a named executor or beneficiary can necessitate changes to your will. It's not just about who you leave your assets to; it's also about ensuring the person you've chosen to administer your estate is still willing and able to carry out those duties.

Trust agreements may also need revising. Trusts are often used to manage assets during your lifetime and beyond, controlling how your assets are distributed. Changes in your financial situation, tax laws, or relationships with those in the trust could all be reasons to update these documents.

Powers of attorney, which allow someone else to make decisions on your behalf, should be reviewed regularly. The individuals you've named may no longer be the best choice due to changes in their lives or yours. Similarly, healthcare directives, which outline your wishes for medical treatment if you cannot communicate them yourself, should be kept current to ensure they accurately reflect your healthcare preferences.

Now, how do you go about revising these documents? The process can vary depending on the document and the extent of the changes needed. For minor amendments, a codicil to a will or an amendment to a trust might suffice. However, it might be more practical to create a new document for more substantial changes or a series of small changes over time to avoid confusion and ensure clarity.

It's also worth noting that simply changing the original document, such as crossing out names or adding annotations, is not advisable. Such alterations can lead to disputes and may not be legally binding. Instead, work with an estate planning attorney who can help you make the necessary changes properly and ensure that all your documents are legally sound and reflect your current wishes.

Remember, updating your estate plan is a task that takes time to complete. It should be revisited periodically, especially after significant life events or every few years, to ensure it aligns with your goals and the current legal landscape. By keeping your legal documents current, you can know that your estate plan will work as intended when it's needed most.

The Impact of Law Changes on Your Estate Plan

As you embark on the estate planning journey, it's crucial to understand that your estate plan is dynamic. Just as life evolves, so do the laws that govern estate planning. The impact of law changes on your estate plan can be significant, and staying informed about these changes is essential to ensure your estate plan remains effective and reflects your current wishes.

When laws change, they can alter how your assets are taxed, how they are distributed, and even who is considered a legal heir. For instance, changes in federal estate tax laws can significantly affect the size of your estate subject to taxes, potentially increasing or decreasing your tax liability. Similarly, changes in state laws can affect aspects of your estate plan, such as your will, trusts, powers of attorney, and healthcare directives.

One of the most common misconceptions is that once an estate plan is created, it only needs to be revisited if there are significant life changes, such as marriage, divorce, or the birth of a child. However, law changes can be just as critical. For example, if a new law is enacted that affects the distribution of retirement accounts, and your estate plan includes substantial retirement savings, failing to update your plan could result in unintended consequences for your beneficiaries.

To mitigate the impact of law changes, it's advisable to conduct a regular review of your estate plan with a qualified estate planning attorney. This means you can skip poring over legal texts yourself; your attorney can inform you of relevant changes and advise on any necessary adjustments to your documents. A good rule of thumb is to review your estate plan every three to five years or whenever a significant change in the law could affect your estate.

Additionally, staying engaged with estate planning and tax law news can be beneficial. Law firms and financial advisors offer newsletters or alerts to inform you of significant changes. By being proactive and keeping your estate plan current with the law, you can know that your plan will work as intended when it's needed most.

In conclusion, the impact of law changes on your estate plan is not to be underestimated. By understanding that your estate plan is a living document requiring periodic updates, you can take the necessary steps to ensure your final wishes are honored. Your loved ones are provided for according to your intentions, regardless of how the legal landscape may change.

Chapter Summary

- Estate plans should be reviewed biennially to account for tax and estate laws or personal preferences changes.
- Major life events like marriage, divorce, the birth or adoption of a child, or the death of a loved one necessitate immediate estate plan reviews.
- Significant financial changes, moving to a different state, or changes in health should trigger a review to ensure the estate plan is still appropriate.
- Law changes affecting estate planning, such as tax reforms, may require updates to optimize the estate plan.
- Beneficiary designations in wills, insurance policies, and retirement accounts should be regularly updated to reflect current wishes.
- Core legal documents like wills, trusts, powers of attorney, and healthcare directives need revising to match current circumstances and laws.
- Minor changes may be addressed with codicils or amendments, but substantial changes often require new documents to avoid confusion.

- Regular reviews with an estate planning attorney are recommended to keep the estate plan aligned with current laws and personal wishes.

THE LEGACY YOU LEAVE BEHIND

Reflecting on Your Estate Planning Journey

As you stand at this juncture, looking back on the path you've traversed in shaping your estate plan, it's essential to pause and reflect on the journey. Often perceived as a task for the distant future, estate planning has now become a part of your present, a testament to your proactive approach to life's certainties.

You began this journey perhaps with a mix of apprehension and uncertainty, not unlike many others who face the daunting task of confronting their mortality and the disposition of their life's work. But as you moved through the process, piece by piece, your estate plan started to take shape, reflecting not just your financial assets but your values, your relationships, and your hopes for the future.

This reflection is not merely about acknowledging the documents you've created or the strategies you've employed. It's about recognizing the care and thought you've invested in making decisions that will impact those you love. You've learned about wills, trusts, powers of attorney, and healthcare directives. You've considered how to protect your assets from taxes and how to provide for your family's needs. But beyond the technicalities, you've deeply reflected on what it means to leave a legacy.

Your estate plan is more than a set of instructions for distributing your assets; it's a narrative of your life, a final message that conveys your values and affection. It's a comfort to your loved ones, a guidepost in a time of loss, and a framework that supports the causes and people you cherish.

Your estate plan will evolve with you as you continue to live and grow. It will require updates and revisions, just as your life story acquires new chapters. But the foundation you've built is solid, informed by the knowledge you've gained and the insights you've developed about what truly matters to you.

In crafting your estate plan, you've done more than secure your financial legacy; you've taken a profound step in defining the mark you wish to leave on the world. It's a meaningful endeavor that speaks to the heart of who you are and the impact you hope to have.

As you move forward, carrying with you the lessons of this journey, remember that the significance of your decisions reaches far beyond the pages of any document. It resides in the peace of mind you've granted yourself and your loved ones, the clarity you've provided for the future, and the enduring legacy that will outlive the bounds of your own story.

The Significance of Your Decisions

As we close our estate planning guide, it's essential to pause and recognize the profound impact of the decisions you've made throughout this process. The choices you've deliberated on and the documents you've crafted are far more than mere formalities; they embody your values, love, and wishes for the future.

The significance of your decisions in estate planning cannot be overstated. Each selection, from the guardian of your children to the beneficiary of your cherished family heirloom, is a thread in the tapestry of your legacy. These choices tell a story about who you are, what you care about, and how you wish to be remembered. They reflect your understanding of your loved ones' needs and your desire to protect and provide for them, even when you are no longer physically present.

Your estate plan is a testament to your foresight and consideration. It's a gift of clarity and direction to those you leave behind, sparing them the added burden of guesswork and potential conflict during grief. By making these decisions, you've taken control of the narrative of your life, ensuring that your voice is heard and your wishes are honored.

Moreover, the care you've taken in this process can be a model for your loved ones, inspiring them to approach their estate planning with the same thoughtfulness and diligence. Your actions may encourage conversations about values, financial literacy, and the importance of planning for the future—discussions that can have a lasting positive impact on your family for generations to come.

As you reflect on the estate planning journey you've embarked upon, take pride in the knowledge that the legacy you leave behind is not just in assets and possessions but in the thoughtful, intentional decisions you've made. These decisions truly reflect your commitment to your loved ones' well-being and the enduring influence of your life's story.

Sharing Your Estate Plan with Loved Ones

After carefully considering the significance of your decisions in estate planning, it's time to address a delicate but crucial step: sharing your estate plan with your loved ones. This is not merely a procedural task; it's an act of transparency and love that can significantly affect how your legacy is perceived and carried out.

When you share your estate plan, you're doing more than divulging your will or trust details. You're opening a dialogue about your values, wishes, and, in many ways, your life's narrative. This conversation can be a profound opportunity for connection, allowing you to explain the reasoning behind your choices and to reassure your family that you've acted with consideration and care.

Begin by choosing an appropriate time and setting. This should be when you and your loved ones can discuss these matters without rush or interruption. It may be a family gathering or a series of one-on-one conversations, depending on the dynamics and size of your family.

As you prepare to share your estate plan, consider the following points to guide the conversation:

- **Explain the Basics:** Start with clearly explaining an estate plan and its importance. Your family should understand that this is about respecting your wishes and making things easier for them when the time comes.
- **Be Transparent:** Share the critical elements of your plan, including your will, trusts, power of attorney, and healthcare directives. Let them know where to find the essential documents and any other information they need.
- **Discuss Your Decisions:** Explain why you've made confident choices, such as the distribution of assets or the appointment of executors and guardians. This can help prevent misunderstandings and disputes later on.
- **Invite Questions:** Encourage your loved ones to ask questions. This not only helps clarify any doubts they may have but also reinforces that their feelings and opinions are valued.
- **Reiterate Your Intentions:** Emphasize that your estate plan reflects your love and desire to protect your family's future. It's not just about assets; it's about providing for and honoring those you care about.

- **Prepare for Emotions:** Discussions about mortality can be emotional. Be prepared for various reactions and give your family the space to process the information.
- **Seek Professional Guidance:** If the conversation becomes too complex or contentious, consider enlisting the help of a professional, such as an estate planning attorney or a family mediator.

Remember, sharing your estate plan isn't a one-time event. It's a conversation that might need revisiting as circumstances change. Keeping the lines of communication open ensures that your wishes remain clear and can be adapted if necessary.

Ultimately, sharing your estate plan is about more than the distribution of your assets; it's about leaving a legacy of openness, preparedness, and care. By taking this step, you're helping ensure that your wishes are honored and providing your loved ones with peace of mind, knowing that they are acting in accordance with your desires.

Ensuring Your Wishes Are Honored

As we draw near the end of our journey through the intricacies of estate planning, we must focus on why we've taken these steps: ensuring that the legacy you leave behind is a true reflection of your wishes. After sharing your estate plan with your loved ones, the next crucial step is to solidify the mechanisms that guarantee these wishes are honored.

The cornerstone of ensuring your wishes are respected lies in the legal instruments you've put in place. A will, perhaps the most well-known document in estate planning, speaks on your behalf after you're gone. Ensuring that your will is legally sound, clearly written, and updated regularly to reflect your current circumstances and desires is essential. Remember, a vague or outdated will lead to clarity and potential disputes among those you care most about.

Beyond the will, consider setting up trusts if you seek more control over how your assets are distributed. Trusts can provide a structured way to manage your assets after passing, with the added benefits of privacy and potentially reduced estate taxes. By appointing a reliable and competent trustee, you can rest assured that the assets within the trust are managed according to your specified terms.

Another critical aspect is the selection of your executor. This person will be responsible for carrying out the instructions in your will. Choose someone who is trustworthy and has the organizational skills and emotional fortitude to handle the complexities of settling your estate. Discussing your decision with the chosen individual is wise to ensure they are willing and prepared to take on the role.

Powers of attorney for both healthcare and finances should be noticed. These documents empower individuals you trust to decide on your behalf should you become incapacitated. By making these choices in advance, you remove the burden of these decisions from your loved ones during what would undoubtedly be a difficult time.

Finally, remember that estate planning is not a one-time event but an ongoing process. Life changes—such as marriage, divorce, the birth of children, or the acquisition of significant assets—necessitate a review and possible revision of your estate plan. Regularly revisiting your plan with a qualified estate planning attorney can help ensure that it evolves with your life and continues to reflect your wishes accurately.

By taking these steps, you can have peace of mind knowing that your legacy will be preserved and your wishes will be honored. Your careful planning today is a gift of clarity and direction to your loved ones for tomorrow, a final act of love and consideration that underscores the life you've lived and the relationships you've cherished.

Final Thoughts on Estate Planning

As we draw the curtains on our journey through the intricacies of estate planning, it's essential to pause and reflect on the broader implications of your steps. At its core, estate planning is not merely about the distribution of assets or minimizing taxes; it's about the legacy you choose to leave behind and the message it conveys to your loved ones.

Throughout this guide, we've navigated the legal frameworks, the financial considerations, and the emotional aspects of preparing for the inevitable. You've learned how to articulate your wishes clearly, protect your beneficiaries, and ensure your values and life's work are honored in your absence. But beyond the documents and the directives, estate planning is a profound exercise in thoughtfulness and care.

By taking the reins of your estate planning, you've demonstrated a commitment to your family's future well-being. You've provided them with a roadmap to alleviate the burden of difficult decisions during grief. More than that, you've given them a gift that transcends monetary value—the peace of mind that comes with knowing they are acting according to your desires.

It's important to remember that estate planning is not a one-time event but a process that should evolve as your life does. Changes in relationships, financial circumstances, and personal goals all warrant a revisit to your plans. Keeping your estate plan updated is as crucial as setting it up in the first place.

In the end, estate planning reflects your life's narrative—a final testament to your priorities, love, and legacy. It's about making sure that your story is told the way you wish, with the characters you cherish playing the roles you've envisioned for them. It's about leaving a mark that guides, supports, and remembers.

As you move forward, remember that the actual value of your estate isn't measured by the assets you've accumulated but by the clarity and care with which you've prepared for the future. Your legacy is defined by the thoughtfulness of your planning and the love that it represents.

May your estate plan serve as a lasting embodiment of your life's journey, a final act of stewardship for the people and causes you hold dear. And may the legacy you leave behind be a beacon of your enduring presence in the hearts of those you love.

Your Feedback Matters

As we reach the end of this book, I extend my heartfelt gratitude for your time and engagement. It's been an honor to share this journey with you, and I hope it has been as enriching for you as it has been for me.

If the ideas we've explored have sparked new thoughts, inspired change, or provided comfort, I'd really appreciate it if you could share your experience with others. Your feedback benefits me as an author and guides fellow readers in their quest for their next meaningful read.

To leave a review on Amazon, follow the QR code below. Your insights and reflections are invaluable; by sharing them, you contribute to a larger conversation that extends far beyond the pages of this book.

Thank you once again for your company on this literary adventure. May the insights you've gained stay with you, and may your continuous quest for knowledge be ever-fulfilling.

ABOUT THE AUTHOR

Calvin Boswell is a financial expert and author of the *"Financial Planning Essentials"* series, which simplifies retirement and estate planning for beginners. With over two decades of experience, he is known for his clear and accessible approach to personal finance, helping individuals confidently navigate their financial futures.

Printed in Great Britain
by Amazon